Adventure Guide

Mazatlan
& Vicinity

Adventure Guide

Mazatlan & Vicinity

Vivien Lougheed

HUNTER

HUNTER PUBLISHING, INC,
130 Campus Drive, Edison, NJ 08818
732-225-1900; 800-255-0343; fax 732-417-1744
www.hunterpublishing.com

Ulysses Travel Publications
4176 Saint-Denis, Montréal, Québec
Canada H2W 2M5
514-843-9882, ext. 2232; fax 514-843-9448

Windsor Books
The Boundary, Wheatley Road, Garsington
Oxford, OX44 9EJ England
01865-361122; fax 01865-361133

ISBN 10: 1-58843-591-1
ISBN 13: 978-1-58843-591-0

Cover photo: Sign, Mazatlan © darrell lecorre/Alamy
Index by: Mary Ellen McGrath

Maps by Kim André, © 2007 Hunter Publishing, Inc.

1   2   3   4

www.hunterpublishing.com

 Hunter's full range of guides to all corners of the globe is featured on our website. You'll find guidebooks to suit every type of traveler, no matter what their budget, lifestyle, or idea of fun.

Adventure Guides – There are now over 40 titles in this series, covering destinations from Costa Rica and the Yucatán to Tampa Bay & Florida's West Coast, Canada's Atlantic Provinces and the Alaska Highway. Complete with information on what to do, as well as where to stay and eat, *Adventure Guides* are tailor-made for the active traveler, with all the practical travel information you need, as well as details of the best places for hiking, biking, canoeing, horseback riding, trekking, skiing, watersports, and all other kinds of fun.

Alive Guides – This ever-popular line of books takes a unique look at the best each destination offers: fine dining, jazz clubs, first-class hotels and resorts. In-margin icons direct the reader at a glance. Top-sellers include *St. Martin & St. Barts*, *The US Virgin Islands* and *Aruba, Bonaire & Curaçao*.

One-of-a-kind travel books available from Hunter include *Best Dives of the Caribbean*, *Cruising Alaska* and many more.

Full descriptions are given for each book at www.hunterpublishing.com, along with reviewers' comments and a cover image. You can also view pages and the table of contents. Books may be purchased on-line via our secure transaction facility.

Contents

TRAVEL INFORMATION

DEDICATION

This book is for Panama Pat Corcoran,
who got me my first review that helped
push me along this path.

Introduction

The lure of isolated beaches rimmed with palm trees brought John Huston to Puerto Vallarta in the 1960s to film *Night of the Iguana*. His cast included Elizabeth Taylor and Richard Burton. While working, the two fell in love. Richard bought Elizabeth a house similar to his own

that was perched on the side of a hill overlooking Bandera Bay. The houses were across the road from each other. The couple then built a walkway between the two places so they could visit each other more discreetly. Elizabeth left Eddie Fisher, her husband at the time, and married Burton. Their story became one of the great love stories of that century.

This romance resulted in thousands of people swarming to the shores of Mexico's west coast in search of sun, sand, palm trees and love. Some even came looking for iguanas. The Mexicans soon realized the potential of tourism and, with the help of international companies, built a first-class infrastructure of hotels, shops and restaurants around the bay.

However, not all visitors wanted what had been built, so they moved up and down the coast to little villages where they could ride horses or donkeys, snorkel among the tropical fish, trek in the jungle looking for exotic birds and animals, watch cliff divers perform or just lay where it was quiet and sip on tequila.

In the jungles along the shore, Mexicans built viewing stations connected by cables where tourists could swing like monkeys while looking for exotic birds and strange amphibians. The usual adjustments took place. Some Mexicans and tourists didn't like the environmental effects caused by chasing around in motorboats looking for big fish, building hotels on the beach, and bungee jumping off bridges. Ecologically-sensitive practices were followed so that wildlife was protected. Garbage was picked up and pollution-control devices were put on vehicles. They left some of the jungle in its wild state and planted flowers in their gardens. More people came.

Today, the west coast of Mexico is as popular as ever. This is because it offers every possible recreational activity, suitable for almost any skill level and budget. The area has both economical and lush accommodations. The food is safe to eat and the bottled water, found in every hotel hallway, grocery store and café is safe to drink. The crime rate is low in tourist areas and the locals are friendly, though the usual pressures of tourism often show. But the best draw of all is that the price for a comparable vacation in any other tropical paradise is about twice what it is here.

The best time to visit the Pacific coast of Mexico is between November and May, when humidity and temperatures are down. This is when most North American and European countries are cold. It is also when the whales move south looking for warmer waters and when the migratory birds are passing by on their way to winter nesting grounds.

But Mexico also has lots to offer during the summer. The Sierra Madres butt up against the ocean, offering relief from the heat just a few hours away by car or public bus. At higher elevations, muscle-powered sports like hiking or cycling are possible any time of year. Museums in the state capitals offer endless intellectual stimulation and the live entertainment often found in towns and city plazas is enthralling. There are ruins to visit and architecture to admire, history to relive and exotic foods to taste.

Herman Melville, the author of *Moby Dick*, was in the Mazatlan area during the late 1800s. There is a plaque commemorating his visit. He loved the place and so will you.

The city of Mazatlan has everything from a Hooters bar to the symphony, golf courses to art museums, sandy beaches with good surf to quiet bays for kayaking. It is divided into three sections. **Old Mazatlan** is at the south end of the bay where the town started to develop for tourism in the 1950s. The center part, **New Mazatlan**, which starts east of Del Mar Avenue, is where new homes, shopping centers and industrial parks have sprouted. The *Zona Dorada*, or **Golden Zone**, is north of Rafael Buelna Avenue, and it's where you'll find big hotels, restaurants, discos, bars and souvenir shops.

HISTORY

Anywhere I go I want to know who was there before me. I want to know their stories.

20,000 BC - Icepack in North America recedes and land bridge is formed between Asia and North America.

12,000 BC - Mesoamerica is populated.

8000 BC -   Nahutal people live on islands near Mazatlan.

5000 BC -   Corn is cultivated in Southern Mexico.

3000 BC -   Pit houses are constructed.

2300 BC -   Pottery replaces stone dishes.

1700 BC -   Olmecs and Totonacs become powerful. They develop hieroglyphics.

600 BC -   Olmecs disappear.

700 AD -   Teotihuacans gain power in Mexico.

1100 AD -   Maya living in Mexico disappear and Aztecs become ruling group.

1517 -   Diego Velasquez and Francisco Fernandez de Cordoba start exploration of Mexico.

Hernando Cortez

1519 -
Aztec chiefs and thousands of civilians are killed by Hernando Cortez.

1528 -
Antonio de Mendoza became the first viceroy of New Spain.

1531 -
Nuño de Guzman and 25 sailors arrive and relieve the locals of their gold.

1535 -   Luis de Velasco becomes a harsh ruler. This is the beginning of 300 years of Spanish rule in America.

1810 -   Miguel Hidalgo inspires peasants to start the War of Independence and on September 16th, won.

1821 -   Agustine de Iturbide declares Mexico a nation with independent rule and himself the emperor.

1824 -   A Constitution is adopted.

1836 -   Antonio Lopez Santa Anna is president and leads war against United States but after his capture, Texas is seceded to the US.

Benito Juarez

1854 -
Benito Juarez overthrew Santa Anna from office and made himself president.

1859-1873
Mazatlan is the capital of the state.

1864 -
French succeed to take over Mexico and put Maximilian into power.

1869 -   Juarez and followers throw Maximilian from power.

1871 -   British occupy bay at Mazatlan.

1876 -   Porfirio Diaz comes to power and the economy flourishes.

1910 -   Francisco I. Madero overthrows Diaz.

1911 -   Victoriano Huerta succeeds Madero after his death.

1914 -   Francisco (Pancho) Villa, Alvaro Obregon, Venustiano Carranza and Emiliano Zapata with the help of the Americans brings down Huerta's government.

1917 -   Present constitution is drawn up.

1928 -   Obregon assassinated.

1930s -   Lazaro Cardenas rules and implements land reform, education for all and he nationalized the petroleum industry.

1940s -   Pan American Highway constructed.

1982 -   Miguel de la Madrid comes to power but due to world oil crises country falls into debt.

1988 -   Carlos Salinas de Gorari wins election and signs NAFTA.

1994 -   Zapatistas capture many small villages in Chiapas.

2000 -   Vincente Fox comes to power under the National Action Party (PAN) putting PRI's 71-year rule to an end.

POLITICAL PARTIES

The three main parties active today are the **National Action Party** (PAN) headed by Vincente Fox, the **Institutional Revolutionary Party** (PRI) that is headed by Francisco Labastida, and the **Party of the Democratic Revolution** (PRD), headed by Cuauhtemoc Cardenas.

States of Mexico

1. Baja California Sur
2. Baja Sur
3. Sonora
4. Chihuahua
5. Sinaloa
6. Durango
7. Coahuila
8. Nuevo León
9. Zacatecas
10. Tamaulipas
11. Nayarit
12. Aquascalientes
13. San Luis Potosi
14. Jalisco
15. Guanajuato
16. Querétaro
17. Hidalgo
18. Veracruz
19. Colima
20. Michoacán
21. México
22. Distrito Federal
23. Tlaxcala
24. Puebla
25. Morelos
26. Guerrero
27. Oaxaca
28. Chiapas
29. Tabasco
30. Campeche
31. Yucatán
32. Quintana Roo

GOVERNMENT

The **United Mexican States** is the official name of the country commonly known as Mexico. The capital of the country is **Mexico City**. Mexico is a federal republic with 31 administrative divisions called states.

MEXICAN STATES

The following is a list of all Mexican states.

Aguascalientes, Baja California, Baja California Sur, Campeche, Chiapas, Chihuahua, Coahuila, Colima, Distrito Federal, Durango, Guerrero, Guanajuato, Hidalgo, Jalisco, Mexico, Michoacan, Morelos, Nayarit, Nuevo Leon, Oaxaca, Puebla, Quintana Roo, Sinaloa, San Luis Potosi, Sonora, Tabasco, Tamaulipas, Tlaxcala, Veracruz, Yucatán, Zacatecas.

OFFICIALS

The government is made up of an executive branch headed by a president, who is both the chief of state and the head of government. The elected government includes a National Congress and a Federal Chamber of Deputies.

The **Cabinet** is appointed by the president after an election, but the assigning of an attorney general requires the consent of the Senate. The **National Congress** is made up of 128 seats, with 96 of those being elected by the people in each district. The 32 non-elected seats are given to members of the elected parties and are proportionally split up according to the number of votes won in the election. This provides for fairer representation. Each member serves a six-year term.

The **Federal Chamber of Deputies** consists of 500 seats, 300 of which are elected by popular vote. The other 200 seats are given to members of the elected parties and, as in Congress, are proportionally split according to the number of votes each party has won in the election. The deputies serve a three-year term.

The **Supreme Court of Justice** is appointed by the president, but must have the approval of the Senate. There are 21 judges who function as the full court or tribunal. Circuit judges and district judges are appointed by the Supreme Court and they must all have law degrees awarded from recognized law schools.

MILITARY SERVICE

Men and women can enter the military at the age of 18 and the forces consist of an army, navy and air force. There are presently almost 200,000 active persons in the military working under an annual expenditure of $4 billion. There are also 300,000 on reserve. It is compulsory for men at the age of 18 to enlist and those 16 years of age may volunteer to receive training as technicians. Women may volunteer at the age of 18. Conscientious objectors are not exempt from service. Which sector of the military one serves is a game of chance. Those who draw a white ball from the bag go into the army or air force, while those who get a blue ball must enter the navy. Mexico offers those in the service an opportunity for secondary education or special training in fields such as social work.

THE POLICE FORCE

Police car.

The Mexican police force is notorious for its corruption. Getting into trouble is usually dealt with by paying a bribe. Because of the low pay, police officers are often people with low education, and many are interested only in expanding their criminal connections. These facts were researched and reported in the *World Policy Journal*, Volume 17, No. 3 in the fall of 2000. The story was also published in *Nexos*, a monthly magazine based in Mexico City, in April and August of 1998. Andrew Reding, a director of the Americas Project at the World Policy Institute, translated the article. For a complete report, go to www.worldpolicy.org/globalrights/mexico/2000-fall-wpj-mexpolice.html.

But there is a good side to the Mexican police force. The **tourist police** found in areas popular with visitors don't seem too corrupt. It appears to me that they have managed to clean up most of the crime in those regions of the country. While walking around I never felt threatened or that I was being watched by potential robbers.

Tourist Police wear red shirts.

However, I still wouldn't take a chance of walking on the beach alone after dark. I also highly recommend that you don't wander around drunk in a public place, that you stay away from the drug trade (of which there is plenty) and that you avoid things like nude bathing except on beaches designated as such. These things are not tolerated and will get you a jail sentence.

Those driving may be stopped and asked for a small contribution, called a *mordida*. Whether you are guilty or not, I suggest you ask for the ticket, or *boleto*. The best that can happen is that the officer will walk away and let you go. The worst that can happen is you will pay a fine for the infraction you have committed. If you pay a traffic ticket within 24 hours, the cost is half.

ECONOMY

Mexico is a free market economy with industry, public services and agriculture owned mostly by the private sector. Tourism is a big draw for the Mexican government and it works hard to attract investors to build the infrastructure tourists require. When visiting the resorts, you will find high-quality rooms, service, food, entertainment and security.

The signing of NAFTA, the **North American Free Trade Agreement**, was done in the hope of improving the economy. According to *The New York Times*, November 19, 2003, the agreement has tripled trade with the US and Canada, but the wages of workers in the manufacturing industry, in agriculture and in the service industry has decreased. The inequality of wages between the middle class and the peasant class has increased, and immigration to the US has continued to rise. The World Bank reports that Mexico has benefitted from the agreement. The main problem seems to be that small farmers, who are no longer subsidized for growing staple crops, have left the farms for the factories, but there aren't enough jobs to go around.

At present, Mexico has free trade agreements with the US, Canada, Guatemala, Honduras, El Salvador and Europe. Over 90% of the country's trading power is under these agreements. In 2002 this increased Mexico's purchasing power to $900 billion, which resulted in a growth rate of 1%.

The **GDP** in 2004 was $1.006 trillion, or $9,600 per person. Of this, 4% came from agriculture, 26.6% from industry, 8.9% from manufacturing, and 69.4% from services. This results in 40% of the population living below the poverty line. Although only 3% of the population is unemployed, there is a huge underemployed group. But it's not all bad. The inflation rate dropped from 52% in 1995 to 6.4% in 2002, the lowest rate in 30 years.

THE MAQUILADORAS

An unpredicted result of the free trade agreements and foreign investment was the emergence of the Maquiladora. Maquiladoras are towns along the Mexican/American border where there are no tariffs on exports. Mexico has few ecological restraints in these areas, so low construction and operation costs are also a big draw. Additionally, the companies can hire cheap labor. The results are cheap goods going back into the rest of North America with no tariffs attached. The backlash of this is that the people of United States and Canada have lost millions of jobs and, in turn, millions of dollars in tax revenue. The Mexican workers living in these towns are underpaid. The results are that the Maquiladoras are huge slums.

Maquiladora children.

PEOPLE & CULTURE

CULTURAL GROUPS

After the Spanish came, it took just two generations to depopulate Mexico of its indigenous peoples. This happened through disease, war and intermarriage. The population is now predominantly *mestizo*, people with a mixture of Spanish and Indian or Negro blood. Today, this group makes up about 60% of the total population. Pure indigenous people are 30% of the population, and whites are about 9%.

There is an unspoken class system that puts the pure European white person at the top. These are the **Creoles**, those born in the country but originating from unmixed European stock. The first Creoles to populate Mexico were the children of the Spanish settlers. Later, they came as refugees from the Spanish Civil War.

Beneath the Creoles on the class scale are the **mestizos** and beneath them are the pure **Amerindians**.

There are also a number of **Asians** in the country, who arrived after they were refused entry into the United States in the late 19th and early 20th centuries. This group shares equal status with the Amerindians.

■ TRADITIONAL ARTS

As of late, a resurgence of cultural pride among cultural groups has resulted in shows of traditional art, theater and dance.

Mexican art includes everything from painted wild fig tree bark to black Oaxaca pottery. Silver and gold have always been a popular medium and the quality of workmanship now found in Mexico is world class. Weavings and carpets have been finding their way into visitors' homes for half a century and the embroidered pieces that can be used as place mats, pillowcases or framed pictures come in colors and designs to accent any décor. Prices for these art pieces are less than half of what you would pay for comparable art in the States.

EMBROIDERY & WEAVINGS

Cotton **rebozos** (ray-BO-zoz), which are handwoven shawls, originated in the Oaxaca area, but can be purchased throughout the western states. This style of weaving, which is rather loose and usually of cotton, is now also being used to make dresses and skirts in fashionable designs that are especially attractive to visitors.

There are embroidered pillowcases or dresser scarves. Some are unique and of high quality, but you must usually hunt for those. Factory-made pieces are far more common and cost much less.

Pine needle **baskets** have been used as containers for everything from food to babies and can be plain, or with geometric, floral or other intricate designs. Though these pieces are not colorful, their beauty lies in the design.

Reeds, on the other hand, are often colored and woven into geometric designs, usually for baskets.

Wool and cotton are used to make the Zapotec handwoven **carpets**. The better ones are made with natural dyes that come from pomegranate, bark, nuts and flowers. They feature intricate geometric designs, like the one shown here, similar to  those on Navajo rugs. The ubiquitous cotton **blankets** woven in simple stripes come in every color and quality.

The weaving of reeds, straw, needles and leaves has been tradition for about 5,000 years. Weavers make things like small mats that are far better for lying upon in the sand than towels.

HUICHOL ART

Huichol art, made with beads, is seen in the shops throughout western Mexico. Some pieces are life-size replicas of animals; others are small. The work is colorful and intricate and depicts images representing stories and deities from Indian myths. Each piece is made by carving the desired shape out of wood or by using a gourd and covering it with a beeswax and pine resin mixture. The colored beads are then placed, one at a time, onto the wood or gourd to create the design.

Huichol art often features animals, like this jaguar piece.

▶▶ AUTHOR TIP: *If you purchase a piece of Huichol art, don't leave it in the sun, as the wax can melt.*

There are many imitations of this art form made in factories with the profits going to the industrialists, rather than artists. To avoid buying factory-made ones, ask if you can purchase another piece exactly the same. If you can, it's a sign that the piece is produced en masse.

LEATHER GOODS

There is a **shoe store** on every street in Mexico. Although you can see the cheap offshore imitations of good quality shoes taking their place on the shelves, there are still many shops that sell the best. Prices are usually a third of what you'll find at home.

And the market isn't restricted to shoes. For reasonable prices, you can purchase purses, belts, jackets, pants, boots, hats and almost anything else that can be made out of leather. The best thing to do if shopping for leather is head to the closest highland town on market day. For example, if staying in Mazatlan, try Tepic. The city is only four hours from the coast.

MASKS

Masks have been worn by traditional dancers for centuries. They can be made out of ceramic, wood, leather or papier mâché and decorated with paint, stones and metals.

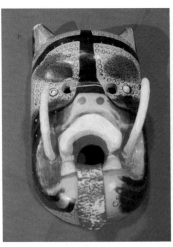
Jaguar mask.

As long as 3,000 years ago, masks were used to imitate gods that had re-incarnated into exotic animals. During the conquest, masks were used to depict oppressors and to emphasize a specific aspect of a story. Now they are used in religious ceremonies and for artistic expression. No matter which mask you purchase, it will be an original.

For an interesting display and brief description of collectors' masks, visit www.mexicanmasks.us.

POTTERY, GLASS & CERAMICS

Pottery and ceramics have been a part of Mexican culture since ancient times, even though many of the religious beliefs that inspired specific works of art have not. Indigenous styles are popular, but the most popular style is **Talavera**, from Arabia via Spain. Talavera pottery is produced only in Puebla. The more Persian-styled works come from Jalisco state. These pieces are usually decorated with gold and silver. If you're in search of something more Mexican-looking, you will be able to find finely decorated ceramic pieces called the "tree of life." They are very ornate and come from post Catholic times.

Tree of Life sculpture.

Stoneware is also common. The most popular piece is a **chess set** made with Aztecs facing conquistadors as opponents. The pieces are usually made of obsidian or onyx.

DRESS

Most mestizo dress like you, in comfortable pants or skirts of the latest fashions (although the women tend to dress on the conservative side). Shorts are worn in the country's western states. Down jackets help keep people warm in the highlands.

On market day or during a fiesta, it is common to see hand-embroidered clothes in myriad colors adorning the Amerindian people.

MUSIC

Mexican music has been popular in European countries as well as the US and Canada since the beginning of the last century. This is probably because of the huge Mexican population in the southern US, especially Texas and California areas, which were once part of Mexico. In recent times, artists like Joan Baez and Linda Ronstadt sang for a large Hispanic audience and popularized Mexican songs like *Gracias a la Vida.*

MARIACHI

Although I often listen to the music of Ronstadt and Baez, for me, Mexican music is the traditional mariachi band. Before the Spanish came, locals used five different instruments to play mariachi. These consisted of various styles of wooden drums and rattles.

After the Spanish arrived, they used music to draw the locals into the Catholic religion. They opened a music school as early as the mid-1500s and introduced such string instruments as the violin, harp and guitar. It didn't take long for the Mexican musician to combine these sounds and make new music not only for the church, but also for fiestas.

By the revolutionary period in the early 1800s, the music had blended traditional Indian tunes with Spanish and Negro tunes. The instruments commonly used were a harp, a violin, a guitar, a drum and a flute. During the battle for independence, music became a unifying symbol. At that time, musicians wore peasant clothing; it wasn't until after independence that they started dressing in what we associate with the Mexican musicians today – tight pants, a black jacket fitted snuggly at the waist, an embroidered belt and a wide bow tie. (See Antonio Banderas in the movie *Desperado.*) On their heads are huge sombreros that were not so

much a symbol of music, but a symbol of wealth (sombreros were once worn only by hacienda owners).

THE CLAIM ON MARIACHI

The word "mariachi" comes from the no-longer-used Coca language of central Jalisco state. However, the French like to think that it comes from the French word *mariage*, and that they gave the word to Mexico. Historical documents indicate that the Coca, not the French, are responsible for the word.

DANCE

Mexican dance is a sensual expression often performed with masks. Before the Spanish arrived, dances depicted the relationship between the gods and mankind. Later, once Christian priests saw the advantage of the enactment, they used dance to stress good and evil in the world according to Christ. However, the Mexicans occasionally used dance as a mockery and to poke fun at the all-powerful forces. The Christians were much too serious to do this.

Each area has its own style of dance. For example, residents of Jalisco dance the jarabe, a romantic display about love and courtship. "Jarabe" means syrup. The dances of Nayarit show the joy of a party and the excitement of becoming an adult. Those in the state of Colima dance after the harvest and their exuberance often includes the throwing of knives. Not, I hope, at one another.

There are numerous **folklorica** shows in all major tourist centers. The acts are usually colorful and fun, and also give an interesting history of the culture and its relationship to the dances you see.

THE LAND

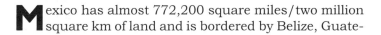

Mexico has almost 772,200 square miles/two million square km of land and is bordered by Belize, Guate-

mala and the US. It has 5,831 miles/9,330 km of coastline.

▨ GEOLOGY

The land forms a bridge between North and South America and consists of high rugged mountains, plateaus,
deserts and low coastal plains. Of these lands, 12% is
farmland, 40% is pasture and 25% is forest and wood-
land.

Within the vegetated hills are plateaus and basins that
form rich valleys like the Atemajac Valley near
Guadalajara. A number of rivers drain these valleys into
the Pacific Ocean.

The American Pacific coast from Alaska down to Tierra
del Fuego is rock interspersed with sandy beaches. Just
offshore, bays are dotted with tiny islands rich with wildlife. There is a limited amount of coral off the coast.

▨ ENVIRONMENTAL CONCERNS

Environmental issues have been a big problem in Mexico. Hotels and cities along the oceans often dump their
raw sewage into the ocean. Water purification plants are
inefficient and below standard. Wildlife has been hunted
almost to extinction. Air pollution is extreme and defor-
estation has resulted in erosion. However, there is a good
side. Tourism is creating a market that demands clean
air, clean water and lots of wildlife. The Mexicans are realizing this and their environmental practices, although
still not up to the standards of places like Switzerland,
are improving. People in the tourist industry are starting
to insist on catch-and-release fishing and no-touch viewing of animals. More people are hiking rather than taking
all-terrain vehicles into the jungle and Mexicans are
putting emissions controls on their vehicles.

The best you can do, as a visitor, is insist on traveling
only with tour companies who are environmentally sensitive. Below are a few of the environmental groups working in Mexico. All are open to enlarging their membership
and their bank accounts.

■ La Systema Nacional de Areas Naturales Protegidas (Sinap) – type in "sinap Mexico" on the Internet and you'll see many references to their programs. Click on one that appeals to you.

■ Audubon Society, www.audubon.org.

■ Greenpeace, www.greenpeace.org.

■ Cetacea Defence, www.cetaceadefence.org.

■ Sea Turtle Survival League, www.cccturtle. org/ccctmp.htm.

■ Earthjustice, www.earthjustice.org.

■ Sierra Club, www.sierraclub.org.

■ World Wildlife Fund, www.panda.org.

PARKS

There are numerous categories for protected public land, but the ones of most interest to travelers are the country's national parks and reserves. National parks are used for recreation or have historical value. These can be large, wild areas with few trails or small parks that are used mainly for strolls. Some feature Maya ruins. Reserves are wildlife sanctuaries or areas set aside for scientific study.

© Tiburonstudios/Dreamstime

Isla Isabel National Park, in Nayarit State, is a tiny island in the Sea of Cortez that has a volcanic crater lake in the center of its 479 acres of land. It is alive with birds. Camping is allowed on the island. See page 186.

CLIMATE

The climate varies from tropical to desert and is dictated the most by elevation. Between November and March, it is warm and dry along the coast. Temperatures run around 26-28°C/80-85°F during the day and drop about 16°C/60°F at night. In Guadalajara (5,000 feet/ 1,500 meters), temperatures average16-21°C/ 60-70°F, with 60% humidity during the day. Nighttime temperatures drop as they do along the coast.

In the wet season, from April to the end of October, the coast experiences around 90% humidity that, coupled with temperatures of over 30°C/90°F, makes walking more than three minutes a huge effort. Guadalajara temperatures average 21°C/75°F during the day, with 80% humidity. This is what locals call the eternal spring climate.

HURRICANES

Because of high temperatures during the wet months (May to November), the water in the ocean heats up, causing a draft sometimes strong enough to create a hur-

Hurricane, seen from space.

ricane. A hurricane forms when there's an area of low pressure in the upper atmosphere and the tropical waters warm to over 26°C/80°F to a depth of 200 feet/60 meters. The heat of the water causes circulation of the winds to accelerate.

The good news is that the west coast does not have as many hurricanes as the Caribbean because most hurricanes move northward in an east-to-west direction. This means that those over the Pacific often miss the mainland because they move toward the ocean. As they move north, the colder temperatures decrease the velocity of the winds. However, the winds and water currents on the swimming and surfing beaches during hurricane season are dangerous.

TSUNAMIS

Since Mexico sits on a tectonic plate, the country is subject to frequent tsunamis. The last one to hit the west coast of Mexico was in 1995, when Manzanillo was struck. Tsunamis can be expected after an earthquake or any other underwater volcanic activity. Occasionally, an underwater mountain will collapse or a landslide will occur and start a wave.

Tsunamis consist of huge waves that are formed far out at sea and can measure up to 90 feet/30 meters in height when they finally hit land. Moving toward land, they can travel as fast as a jet liner, up to 500 mph/800 kmph. They can move back and forth across the ocean for hours, over distances of up to 12,000 miles/19,000 km, before they finally peter out.

FACT FILE: *A 1960 tsunami that started near Chile killed 150 people in Japan 22 hours later.*

DEADLIEST RECORDED TSUNAMIS IN THE AMERICAS		
Location	**Date**	**Lives lost**
Chile	May 22, 1960	1,260
Colombia/Ecuador	Dec. 12, 1979	500
Venezuela	Jan. 31, 1906	500
Guatemala/El Salvador	Feb. 26, 1902	185
Nicaragua	Sept. 2, 1992	170
Aleutian Islands	Apr. 1, 1946	165
United States (Alaska)	Mar. 28, 1964	123
Chile	Nov. 11, 1922	100
Mexico	June 22, 1932	75
Canada (Newfoundland)	Nov. 18, 1929	51
Solomon Islands	Oct. 3, 1931	50

Tsunamis, when they reach land, throw the sediment from the ocean floor over a half-mile/one km inland; once the water subsides, this sedimentation can be over three feet/one meter deep. Tsunamis cause terrible destruction to the vegetation along the coast and often destroy entire villages.

When a tsunami approaches shore, it appears as a wall of water. A tsunami wave does not crest.

EARTHQUAKES

Earthquakes in the central and south region of the country are common. The one that hit Mexico City on September 19, 1985 had a magnitude of 8.1 on the Richter Scale and was the worst to hit since the Great Jalisco quake of 1932. Quakes occur when tectonic plates under the earth's surface move. When the quake hit Mexico City, the tectonic plate moved seven feet/2.5 meters across and 32 in/80 cm in a vertical direction. When an earthquake occurs under manmade structures, the damage is immense. The 1985 quake covered an area of almost 5,405 square miles/14,000 square km. It caused a tsunami that hit the coast from Manzanillo to Acapulco, causing most damage in the town of Zihuatanejo, where the wave was 10 feet/three meters high.

The aftershock of the Mexico City earthquake hit two days later and measured 7.5 on the Richter Scale, but that occurred 60 miles/100 km from the main site. It too, caused some tsunami activity.

PLANT LIFE

When we think of the Pacific coast of Mexico, we see swaying palms along sandy beaches and bougainvillea hanging over stone fences. Panning the landscape a bit farther inland we see giant cactus and spiked shrubs; lizards and snakes skittering around the dry ground. In the higher elevations, we see lush rainforest with canopies so solid they hide the sun and the parrots, monkeys, scorpions and snakes that live there.

ECOLOGICAL ZONES

The flora can be described in terms of seven distinct ecological zones between the Pacific coast and the highlands of Guadalajara or Mexico City. Each zone supports a huge variety of plants, animals, birds, amphibians and reptiles. The ocean has a vast array of vegetation, corals, mammals and fish. It is beyond the scope of this book to describe the entire natural habitat of western Mexico but, for the beginner, below are a few of the common characteristics of this unique environment.

TROPICAL DECIDUOUS FOREST

A tropical deciduous forest follows the west coast from the north to the south. It contains such plants as the palm tree (of which there are about 3,000 species worldwide), strangler fig or *mato palo* (in Spanish), pink trumpet tree (highly poisonous), cardinal sage, spider lily and the *mala raton* (bad rat). These plants usually lose their leaves during the dry season and flower between May and September, during the rainy season.

The **palm tree**, so common in the tropical deciduous forest, has been used for everything from baking ingredients to home construction to basket weavings to the promotion of paradise. The ones seen on the coast are usually the coconut or fan palm. The coconut palm is tall, with green-husked fruit clustered near the base of the fronds. You can recognize the palm that produces palm oil by the thousands of crab apple-sized nuts hanging below the fronds. On the fan palm, each leaf

Strangler fig.

looks like a huge fan. The **strangler fig** is often associated with Tarzan and the deep jungle. This plant is a parasite that winds itself around a host tree and eventually sucks all the nutrients out of its captive. The strangler has numerous aerial roots that hang down from the host. Some of these roots can be quite thick and are strong enough to swing upon.

The **pink trumpet**, with its huge bell-shaped flowers that hang from every limb, is beautiful to look at but deadly to eat. **Cardinal sage**, also known as *Salvia fulgens*, should not be confused with *Salvia divinorum*, a hallucinogenic plant that was once used by shaman of the Oaxaca region for religious purposes. The cardinal version grows about three feet (one meter) in height, has red flowers and seems to be especially attractive to hummingbirds. When the Spanish arrived, the **spider lily** could be found growing near the swamps of Mexico City and has since spread to the swamps of the Pacific coast. The flower clusters grow in all shades of red, from light pink to deep maroon, and are found on leafless stems. The bulbs are poisonous. A sister plant to the Mexican variety grows in Japan and is planted at the entrances to temples.

PACIFIC THORN FOREST

The Pacific thorn forest is located around Mazatlan, south of Puerto Vallarta and between Manzanillo and Ixtapa. This vegetation zone, located in a fairly dry environment, includes such plants as the morning glory tree, the acacia, the mimosa, the fishfuddle tree and the candelabra cactus. Because of the climactic dryness, these plants are generally scrub or cactus-like in appearance.

The **morning glory tree** grows to about 30 feet/10 meters in height. Its cream-colored flowers are about two inches wide with bright red centers.

THE ROOT OF THE PROBLEM

The morning glory tree is also called *Palo del Muerte* (Tree of Death) or *Palo Bobo* (Fool Tree) because it was believed long ago that if one drank the water that flowed near the roots of the tree, he would either die or go crazy.

The **mimosa**, of which there are about 2,500 varieties, is often associated with the dry lands of Africa. However, some types can be found along Mexico's Pacific coast. They can grow as high as 35 feet/10 m, with a foliage spread of about the same. In some places the mimosa is known as the shaving brush tree because of its delicate thread-like flowers that resemble a shaving brush.

The **acacia** is similar to the mimosa in that its leaves are six to 12 inches long with anywhere from 11 to 23 leaflets attached symmetrically to a single stem. The thorn acacia has a double thorn at the base of the leaf stem and houses ants that bite any possible intruders. In return for this protection, the plant provides nourishment to the ant. The thorns were once used as sewing needles by those living in the area. The yellow clusters of flowers that appear in May are highly scented and leave a seedpod that is often eaten by birds.

© Manicblue/Dreamstime

In spring, the acacia sports clusters of yellow flowers.

The **candelabra cactus** looks like its name suggests, except it always has more than the seven branches (the candleholders). The plant grows three-12 feet/one-four meters high. Its branches have six to eight ribs and a long central spine. When the skin is ruptured, the plant oozes a milky sap that is poisonous to humans.

SAVANNAH

The savannah or plains grasslands are common in the state of Sorora and farther east. These semi-desert areas are often called *pastizales* (pastures) and are characterized by the abundant grasses (usually bunchgrass) that grow there. However, shrubs and small trees also flourish. The hot, dry climate receives less than 12 in/30 cm of rain a year and often has daytime temperatures of over 100°F/38°C. Over 700 invertebrate species make this environment their chosen home.

MESQUITE GRASSLAND

Generally, this land has been overgrazed, causing damage to the grassland. Mesquite grassland is where the **mescal cactus** is grown. There are numerous species of mescal grown and used in Mexico, but the most famous is the one from which tequila is made. It comes in two varieties, the agave tequelana and the aguey azul. In and around Guadalajara, Tequila and Tepatitlan huge plantations (a total of 62,000 acres is presently under cultivation) produce the aguey azul. These plants ripen in about six years, at which time the leaves are hacked away and the heart of the plant is chopped and roasted. It is then shredded and pressed, sugars and yeast are added and it is left to ferment. After fermentation, the liquid is distilled and we get to enjoy a delicious margarita.

PINE-OAK FORESTS

FACT FILE: *Forty percent of vertebrates known to live in Mesoamerica make the pine-oak forests their home, including the canyon tree frog. This is one of Mexico's most endangered ecosystems at present.*

The pine-oak forests of the Sierra Madres hold many endangered species. This ecosystem lies between 4,500 and 7,500 feet/1,400 and 2,300 meters in elevation and trees here grow to a height of 75-125 feet/25-40 meters. Pine-oak regions usually have a thick undergrowth that includes ferns and water lilies, many of which are endangered.

CLOUD FORESTS

Cloud forests or rainforests are defined as areas that receive 160-400 in/400-1,000 cm of rain annually and have little temperature change throughout the year.

> **FACT FILE:** *All of the world's rainforests lie between the Tropic of Cancer and the Tropic of Capricorn and are on land that has never been glaciated. This may be the reason that rainforests play host to such a huge number of different species.*

Typically, trees in the rainforest grow over 150 feet/45 meters and their branches spread out, forming a lush canopy over the creatures living below. This canopy prevents most of the sunlight from reaching the forest floor, leaving the ground with few nutrients. Since the root systems of these trees must compete for the small amount of available nutrients, roots spread out sideways rather than heading deep down into the ground. This type of growth leaves trees somewhat unstable. To counter this instability, many trees, such as the ceiba, have developed buttresses at the base of their trunks that act like stabilizing arms. Long woody vines called **lianas** are common in the cloud forest, as are orchids and bromeliads, or air plants. **Orchids** are members of the most highly evolved plants on the planet. There are about 25,000 species worldwide. Their evolution

Orchid.

has developed thick leaves that hold moisture for the plant. Some of the flowers are highly perfumed to attract creatures for pollination. The vanilla is the most aromatic of the orchids.

The pineapple is the most commonly known bromeliad.

Similar in appearance to the orchids are **bromeliads**, plants of the pineapple family. Unique to the Americas, bromeliads will grow in any elevation up to 8,000 feet/2,500 meters and anywhere from rainforest environment to desert. Also like orchids, these plants gather nutrients and moisture in their leaves; their roots serve only as anchors and are not used to gather food. Some bromeliads are as small as one inch across, while others grow to three feet.

TROPICAL REGIONS

This moist environment below 1,500 feet/500 meters has many **heliconias**, plants like the ginger, bird of paradise, prayer plant and banana. These plants all have

Bird of Paradise.

large leaves and brilliant flowers. Banana trees (not actual trees, but heliconias) are abundant in Mexico. The fruits of different species vary; some are tiny, some large, some sweet and some bitter. You'll often see banana stalks hanging from trees wrapped in blue plastic bags designed to protect the fruit from insects. After the fruit stalk is removed from a tree, the treetop is chopped off and left at the base as fertilizer. New shoots grow and, eight months later, a new stalk of bananas is growing on the new tree.

NOPAL CURES

Nopal is a plant that has been eaten for thousands of years. Its fruit comes in different colors and tastes like watermelon or raspberries or pears, depending on the color. The green leaf is used in herbal medicines to cure diabetes, kidney infections and burns. The fruit is also used in salads and soups.

ANIMAL LIFE

The wildlife in Mexico is making a comeback after years of abuse – over-hunting of animals, over-grazing of grasslands, over-logging of forests and over-fishing of waters. Because tourists are more interested in whales and dolphins than in marinas, Mexicans are cashing in and again trying to give the tourists what they want. Parks and reserves are numerous and locals are relentless in their attempts to educate people about the environment.

Mammals common to the country are armadillos, coatis, spider monkeys and jaguars. Coyotes are numerous, as are rabbits, squirrels and deer. Reptiles include crocodiles, turtles, snakes and lizards. There is no greater thrill than to walk alone in the jungle and see a huge reptile slither away to the safety of the bush as you pass by. On the other hand, there is nothing more frightening than to come across the aggressive

Jaguar.

fer-de-lance snake while walking in the jungle.

Marine life is also rich, with gray and humpback whales, dolphins, swordfish, sailfish, marlin and roosterfish. There are many sportfishing operators who practice catch and release. The photos so common a few years ago of a dozen sailfish next to the proud white hunter are no longer popular.

ON LAND

RODENTS

There is the usual array of rodents, including the **squirrel, gopher, rat, rabbit** and **porcupine**. Distinct for their

Porcupine.

gnawing abilities, these animals have teeth that never stop growing and must be worn down in order for the animal to survive. Rodents are generally small and eat mostly vegetation, although their diets are often supplemented with eggs, birds and insects. Rodents are also a highly reproductive group, having at least one and sometimes numerous litters every year. **Audubon's ground squirrel** is seen near the beaches. Yellowish-brown in color, these two-foot-long, short-necked rodents live underground and are both gregarious and social. They live in underground communities, eat insects, fruits and grasses and usually have five kids per litter. They store food in ground holes and their keen sense of smell allows them to find the food again. The **Colima squirrel** is gray, with large eyes and small flexible ears. It grows up to three feet/one meter long, including the tail. Colima squirrels like to live in mango plantations and palm groves, where they feast on the fresh fruits. These sociable animals live in groups of 10 to 12 adults. Each female will give birth to about five kids, which she keeps close for eight to 10 weeks.

BATS

Bats are the only mammals that fly. In the Americas, bat wingspans range in size from a tiny three in/seven cm to six feet/two meters. There are over 1,000 types of bats in the world and Mexico has its fair share.

The wing of the bat is like a webbed hand, with a thumb and four fingers. It is used to scoop up food, cradle young or hug itself for warmth. Bats like their own homes and live an average lifespan of 30 years in the same cave, near the same hanging spot. All bats in a cave are related, except for one reproducing male who always comes from another family and area. The females give birth to one baby a year, but the infant mortality rate is high, up to 60%. During the first year of life, the mothers leave their babies only when hunting for food. When they return to the cave, they call to their young, who recognize their parent's sounds and answer. Following the sound, the mother joins her youngster.

FACT FILE: *Bats can eat up to 3,000 insects in one sitting and up to 1,000 mosquitoes in an hour. I don't know who does the counting but, if the figures are correct, I really like bats.*

CATS

JAGUAR: Jaguars are the largest and most powerful cats in the Americas. Often referred to as *el tigre*, the jaguar stands 20-30 in/50-75 cm at the shoulder and has an overall length of six-eight feet/two-three meters. Its slender but strong body can weigh 250 lb/115 kg. The jaguar is built to hunt, with strong shoulders, sharp teeth, good eyesight and hearing, and claws that can rip the hamstring of a deer with one swipe. The jaguar's short fur is usually yellow with black spots, or black circles with a yellow dot in the center. Some jaguars appear all black, but it is just that the black circles are so big they override any trace of yellow. There is no specific breeding season for the jaguar. Both parents care for the kitten for about one year after birth, at which time everyone splits and fends for themselves. With good luck and lots of food, the jaguar lives about 20 years.

PUMA: The red tiger, or puma, is also called the mountain lion, cougar or panther. Just a bit smaller than the jaguar, this animal lives throughout North and South America wherever deer, its main source of food, is found. Comparable in strength to the jaguar, the puma can haul an animal five times its size for a considerable distance. When hunting, it strikes with lightening speed and can spring forward 25 feet/7.5 meters in one leap and jump down 60 feet/18 meters to land safely. Like the jaguar, the puma can mate at any time of year and both parents help look after the young. The puma's life expectancy is 15 years.

COATI: The coati is a tree-climbing mammal related to the raccoon. It has a long snout (tipped white) and an even longer tail that is usually the same length as its body. It keeps its striped tail high and, as it walks, the tail swings from side to side. Coatis are sociable animals and the females often travel with their young in groups of up to 20. When a group of these animals attacks a fruit tree, they often devour the entire crop in a few minutes. A full-grown male stands 10 in/25 cm at the shoulder and will grow to two feet/50 cm long. As this omnivore hunts both in the day and at night and eats just about anything, you have a good chance of seeing one moving along in tall grass or along rocky hillsides.

© Photographer: Ramon Berk/Dreamstime

MONKEYS

Spider monkeys have grasping hands that have no functional thumbs and a grasping tail that is hairless at the end. These five "hands" make the spider monkey efficient in maneuverability. They travel in bands of 20 to 30 and will attack threatening invaders. They use fruits and branches as weapons and have been known to urinate on enemies walking below. There are signs in Manuel Antonio Park, Costa Rica, warning tourists of this possibility.

AMPHIBIANS

Amphibians include **frogs**, **toads**, **newts**, **salamanders**, **sirenians** (sea cows) and **caecilians** (creatures that look like earthworms). Although amphibians have lungs, they also do some air exchange through their skin. They are found worldwide, except on the poles and in extreme deserts. Amphibians are hatched from eggs and usually go through a tadpole or larvae stage, where breathing is done through gills. They metamorphose and then use lungs. Their skins are moist, glandular and pigmented, although if living away from light, pigmentation is mini-

Sticky frog.

mal. Some, like the salamander, are able to rejuvenate lost body parts (for some reason, the back end of the creature is quicker to respond to re-growth than are the front limbs). The most endearing feature of the amphibian is its ability to consume large amounts of insects, especially mosquitoes.

REPTILES

Reptiles are prominent in Mexico and it would be a rare visit if you didn't see at least one iguana, snake, turtle, or gecko while there. Reptiles control their temperature by moving in their environment. If it is too hot in the sun, they move to the shade. They all have a tough dry skin that is used primarily to preserve body moisture.

SNAKES: The **fer-de-lance** is the most dangerous of Mexico's snakes and its bite is usually fatal. It is an aggressive, nocturnal viper that can be found almost anywhere – in a tree, on the jungle floor, in the grass or out in the open. Its markings are not distinct, so it is hard to identify. It has an arrow-shaped head and a mouth with two retractable fangs appearing too big for the snake's head. The fer-de-lance comes in many colors, from dark brown to gray to red, and has a row of dark-edged diamonds along its sides.

> **WARNING:** If you are attacked by one of these snakes, you must get to a doctor immediately. Twenty-four hours is too long to wait; some people say that you have only 20 minutes to receive treatment before you die.

The **rattlesnake**, found only in North America, is in danger of becoming extinct. Identified by the rattle sound made by the animal shaking its tail, rattlers are not as dangerous as the fer-de-lance, although their bite can be fatal. If bitten, you should see a doctor who will administer some antivenin, a drug obtained from horses that neutralizes the snake's venom.

FACT FILE: *More people die every year in the US from bee and wasp stings than from snake bites.*

Coral snakes are nocturnal, but are far less aggressive than the fer-de-lance and are hard to find as they like to hide in ground vegetation. They also prefer eating other snakes, rather than sharpening their teeth on you. However, if you step on one and are bitten, get to a doctor immediately as they are one of the most poisonous snake in the tropics.

The yellow-bellied sea snake is a carnivorous snake that seldom grows over 45 in/ 113 cm. It hunts fish during the day. The snake sleeps on the ocean floor, rising to the surface once every one to three hours to breathe. It is mild-mannered and often

Yellow-bellied sea snakes can swim at speeds of up to 2 mph.

swims in groups of up to a hundred. If washed ashore by wave action, it has a hard time getting back to the water and it often dies. Sea snakes expel only a small amount of poison when they bite. If bitten, your life is not in danger, but you should still see a doctor.

TURTLES: The green turtle is so named because of the color of its fat. The black turtle is a subspecies of the green. These slow-growers do not reach sexual maturity until 20 years of age, and some take up to 50 years. The green turtle will grow to 39 in/one meter and weigh about 330 lb/150 kg. In the recent past, these creatures would grow to twice that size. Today, we harvest them so rapidly that they no longer have time to grow.

The green turtle is vegetarian and likes to graze on meadows of sea grass that grow in warm ocean waters. However, immature greens are known to eat a bit of meat. The females nest once every two to four years. Each nesting season results in two or three breeding sessions that are about 14 days apart. The female lays about 100 eggs each time and the young hatch 60 days later. The largest known nesting beach is at Colola in the state of Michoacan.

Green sea turtle resting on a coral reef full of fishes.

© Pufferfishy/Dreamstime

Leatherback turtles are in great danger of extinction worldwide. This is the largest living turtle, growing up to 110 in/270 cm long and weighing up to 2,000 lb/900 kg. The leatherback is so named because it has a flexible shell that resembles leather. There is no separation from the sides of the shell and the underbelly, so it appears a bit barrel-shaped. An old study from the early 1980s found that of all the leatherbacks known to exist worldwide, almost half of them nested on the western shores of Mexico. However, more recent studies have indicated that the turtles travel to Japan to nest and, when the young hatch, sea currents return the babies to the western shores of America. One of the greatest threats to the leatherback is that it mistakes plastic bags and Styrofoam pollutants for food. Once the garbage is ingested, the turtle's gut becomes blocked, nutrition is limited and death is close.

The **Olive Ridley turtle** is the most abundant turtle in the Pacific Ocean. It is small, merely 22-30 in/56-76 cm long. Some of the females nest in arribados, or groups. The grouping of turtles is believed to have evolved so they can help each other protect their eggs.

THE WAITING GAME

Some turtles have been known to stay in the water waiting for a safe moment to lay their eggs and, while waiting, the eggs develop hard shells. When the turtle eventually tries to lay her eggs, they are very difficult to pass and, because of the rigidity, they break.

The Ridley turtle nests every year, three to four times during each season, as opposed to the green turtle who has a nesting season only every two to four years but nests three times each season. It takes 14 days for eggs to hatch from the females who nest alone, and up to 28 days for the arribado nesters. Only 5% of eggs actually produce offspring. One scientific theory for this is that 90-95% of the eggs produced are unfertilized (without a yolk) and left at the top of the nest so predators will eat them and not bother with the fertilized eggs lying below. Olive Ridley turtles are omnivorous and include crab, shrimp, lobsters, jellyfish, algae and sea grasses in their diets.

INSECTS

Insects and arachnids include mosquitoes and cockroaches, botflies and butterflies, houseflies and fireflies, fire ants and leaf-cutter ants, termites and scorpions. Some bite and others don't. Some are good to eat (like ants, which you can cover in chocolate) and some are not even wanted by birds, toads or frogs (like fireflies). Below I have mentioned just a few of the more interesting ones.

Scorpions should be avoided because they do bite; shake out shoes and clothes before putting them on when in the jungle. Apparently, the smaller the scorpion the more lethal its bite.

For the most part, **ants** work in the service industry, cleaning up garbage left around the jungle floors (and your room, if you are careless). Highly organized, their hills can measure many feet across and be equally as high. A colony of leaf-cutter ants (also called wee-wee ants) can strip a full-grown deciduous tree within a day. These ants chew and swallow the leaves, which they regurgitate shortly after. The vomit grows a fungus, which the ants then eat for nutrition. The excretion left by the ants helps to fertilize the jungle floors. The ants' colonies consist of females only and the queen is the size of a small mouse. Her job is to lay eggs; she has workers to clean and feed her.

There are hundreds of species of **butterflies** and **moths** in Mexico and their colors and designs are fascinating. Some have eye markings at their tail end (to fool predators as to the direction they will be going), while others are so bright they attract the attention of all. Butterflies and moths have no jaws, so they don't bite. Instead, they suck up nutrients in liquid form. For protection from rain, high winds and extreme heat, they sit on the undersides of leaves.

OTHER BEASTS

Skunks are often incorrectly referred to as polecats. A polecat is native only to Europe and Asia; skunks are found in America anywhere from northern Canada all the way down to Patagonia. Related to the weasel, the skunk is able to spray a foul-smelling substance a distance of 12 feet/3.5 meters. The skunk actually aims for the eyes of its enemy. The liquid produces temporary blindness in the recipient. A night hunter, the skunk comes out of its den when the temperatures cool and it forages for insects, larvae, mice and fallen fruits. Skunks mate in spring and have litters of five or six young that are ready to look after themselves after about two months. Their life span is around 10 years.

© Jeff Dean
Peccaries cannot be tamed.

The **peccary** is a pig-like creature that has been around for about 40 million years (according to fossil finds). Not very big, it weighs about 65 lbs/30 kg and travels in herds of a few individuals to as many as 300. The peccary has two distinct features. One is the smell it exudes from a musk gland on its back whenever it is irritated. The second is its amazing nose, the tip of which is flat and reinforced with a cartilaginous disk that can lift logs and dig underground for roots and insects. A true omnivore, the peccary will eat anything from poisonous snakes to cactus. There is no fixed mating season and the female usually gives birth to one or two young about the size of a full-grown rabbit. By the time the young are two days old, they are ready to take their place in the herd.

The **armadillo** is an insect-eating mammal that has a bony-plated shell encasing its back. This shell is the animal's protection. The armadillo has  teeth that are simple rootless pegs in the back of its mouth. Because of these teeth, the armadillo is able to eat snakes, chickens, fruit and eggs. It also likes to munch on the odd scorpion. The female gives birth to a litter of young that are all the same sex; the theory is that they develop from the same egg. The young are born with shells, but the shells don't harden until the animal is almost a year old. This is when it leaves its mother.

AIRBORNE

BIRDS

Because Mexico lies on the migratory path, seeing both common and rare bird species is possible, often in larger numbers than elsewhere. Numerous bird tours come to this area from the United States. Many environmental groups are involved in preserving areas that the birds use so their numbers are again increasing. If you have more than a passing interest in birds, bring your favorite identifying book and binoculars with you.

Parrots are brightly plumaged, gregarious creatures that have no problem imitating human speech. They will be the most ubiquitous bird (next to the frigate and pelican) you will see. In total, there are 358 parrot species worldwide. Along with bright colors, all parrots have strong hooked beaks with moveable upper jaws and thick tongues. They eat fruit and seeds. Captive parrots make strong bonds with their owners and are known to become physically ill if abandoned. The species most commonly seen on Mexico's west coast are the tiny (four-six inch/ 10-15 cm) Mexican parakeet, the orange-fronted parakeet, the lilac-crowned parrot and the military macaw.

Frigatebird looking for a mate.

The **frigate** is the big, black bird you see soaring over the water with a "W" shaped wing. It can soar for hours over the sea, although it seldom goes more than 50 miles/80 km from its home island. Because it does not lift off from water very well, it doesn't fish much. Instead, it steals from other birds or swoops down and catches fish swimming near the surface.

To attract a female at for mating, the male frigate puffs his large red throat.

Pelicans come in eight varieties, the most common of which is the brown pelican. Their pouch bills could easily hold a newborn human. Their bodies are about 40 in/ 100 cm long and their wingspan is a mighty 90 in/ 228 cm. These birds, when fishing, torpedo into the water from great heights. Their ancestors can be traced back about 40 million years, but in the 1950s and 1960s pelicans almost disappeared from earth due to DDT poisoning. They are now making a comeback. Each female lays about three eggs per year and the hatchlings are born four weeks later.

The **cara cara**, Mexico's national bird, is a raptor with black and white plumage and a featherless face. Its legs are bare and its tearing beak is hooked like an eagle's and long like a vulture's. It an indiscriminate scavenger and will eat garbage, dine with both eagles and vultures, or kill its own dinner. Cara caras love to eat anacondas, boa constrictors and caimans. When they leave the nest, the young are 21 in/55 cm long, with a four-foot/1.3-m wingspan. Due to loss of savannah and wetlands, the bird is endangered, but that is just part of the problem. Throughout Central and South America, their claws were used for jewelry and their feathers used to make ceremonial robes for priests. More recently, claws and beaks have been ground and sold as aphrodisiacs. The use of DDT in the last 25 years has also taken its toll on the development of eggs. Cara caras are slow reproducers.

RECOMMENDED BIRDING BOOKS

The most comprehensive tome available is the ***Field Guide to the Birds of Mexico and North Central America***, by Steve Howell and Sophie Wedd, published by Oxford Illustrated Press. It has color plates and black-and-white drawings that illustrate 750 species. It has 1,010 pages and is heavy to carry.

Mexico: A Hiker's Guide to Mexico's Natural History, by Jim Conrad, Mountaineer Books in 1995. This 220-page book combines wildlife information with 20 trail descriptions.

Bird-Finding Guide to Mexico, by Steve NG Howell, Cornell University Press, 1999. The book's 512 pages describe 100 sites where birders may see more than 950 species.

Birds of Mexico and Adjacent Areas, by Ernest Preston Edwards, University of Texas Press, 3rd edition, 1998. Lists 870 species, with 300 that are not included in other guides. The names include English, Spanish and the scientific names.

▨ IN THE OCEAN

Dolphins are playful and intelligent. They mature between five and 12 years and a female gives birth to one calf every two or three years. The life span of a dolphin is up to 48 years. Dolphins travel in pods and it is suspected that each member of a pod is related. They like to stay near their home waters for their entire life. They hunt for fish using the echolocation method similar to bats. A dolphin will eat up to 150 lb/68 kg of fish a day.

Hammerhead sharks are one of nine species of sharks. They grow anywhere from three feet/one meter to 20 feet/six meters, but most average 11.5 feet/four meters long. They weigh around 500 lb/230 kg, but can weigh up to 1,000 lb/450 kg. They kill their prey by smashing them with their heads and they especially like to eat squid, rays, crustaceans and each other. They generally swim at a depth of 250 feet/75 meters, migrating north in summer and south in winter. Females give birth to 20 to 40 live pups that are about 27 in/70 cm long.

WHALES: Great gray whales migrate down the Pacific coast from the Arctic waters each year around October and return the following spring around May. The gray whale belongs to the baleen whale classification because it has baleen, a substance made of keratin similar to fingernails, instead of teeth. The baleen grows in strips down from the upper jaw.

> **FACT FILE:** *There can be up to 180 plates of baleen on each side of a whale's or shark's jaw. The strips grow two-10 in/five-25 cm and, since the ends wear down from eating, they must continue to grow during the animal's entire life.*

Baleen is used to filter amphipods from the ocean bottom. Land deposits due to erosion of the earth along the oceans cause death to these tiny bottom growers and results in the grays having to go farther afield in search of food. An average-size gray measures 40-50 feet/12-15 meters long and weights up to 40 tons. Grays are known to live about 50 years, are gray in color and have scars caused from barnacles. It is also common to see orange whale lice growing on their skin. Gray whales have 10-12 dorsal nodules rather than fins and their tails are 10 feet/three meters across. Grays have hair, are warm-blooded and suckle their young for six months. During the suckling period, babies drink around 50 gal/200 liters of milk a day, gaining 50 lb/23 kg of body weight per day.

A female must be 36-39 feet/nine-10 meters in length before she is mature enough to mate. A 15-foot/five-meter), one ton/1,000 kg calf is born a year later. During delivery, a second female may help with the birthing by holding the mother up near the surface so she can breath. After birth, the youngster does some practice swims back and forth against the current in preparation for the 10,000-km/6,000-mile migration north.

Humpback whales also belong to the baleen classification of mammals. They, too, have patterns on their dorsal fins and tails that are as unique as fingerprints on humans. Humpbacks are black on top and white on their bellies, have irregular-shaped dorsal fins and tails that can be up to 18 feet/5.5 m wide. They are usually 40-50 feet/12-15 meters in length and weigh 25-40 tons. They feed on small crustaceans and fish. Humpbacks can consume a ton of food every day.

Humpbacks "lunge-feeding."

Humpbacks reach maturity when they are 36-39 feet/ 11-12 meters long, which is usually reached by six to eight years of age. Females have a calf once every two to three years and the gestation period is one year. The calf weighs around a ton at birth and suckles for a year. Humpbacks, like gray whales, migrate north in summer and return south to mate and give birth in winter.

SPORTFISH: Swordfish are part of the billfish family and are identified mainly by their long sword-like upper jaws.

They have large eyes, brown bodies with white bellies and have no scales or teeth. They have been known to grow up to 200 lb/90 kg but, due to over-harvest, are now much smaller. They like to eat other fish, squid and octopus.

Sailfish are also part of the billfish family and have a large upper jaw that looks like a spear. But it is the en-larged dorsal fin that gives the fish its name. Sailfish grow to four-five feet/one-two meters in their first year of life and usually reach seven feet/two meters and 120 lb/60 kg at maturity. The sailfish is a fast swimmer, often traveling up to 50 knots.

Blue and **black marlin** are more often found in the At-lantic than the Pacific. However, those in the Pacific grow to 14 feet/four meters and can weigh one ton/900 kg. The largest marlin found in the Pacific was 1,376 lb/624 kg. Marlin eat dolphin, tuna and mackerel. Spawning season is May to November, and the eggs hatch about one week after being deposited. The marlin's biggest predator is the white shark, but man, too, has over-fished this species. The catch-and-release practice of fishing has not been so good for this group because the damage occurred during the catch usually kills the fish.

The **rooster fish** has a spiked dorsal fin with eight thorns. It is gray-blue in color, with a silver underbelly and two dark spots, one on the nose and another on the nape of the neck. It likes to swim near shore where there is a sandy bottom and is also found around reefs. Rooster fish usually grow to 10 in/25 cm long and weigh about 115 lb/55 kg. Because of their great fighting abil-ity, they are a desired sportfish.

Dorado is also called mahi mahi or dolphin. It has a flat face, large dorsal fin and is a metallic blue-green in color with orange-gold specks. It is grows from 15-30 lb/five-12 kg and eats mainly smaller fish. The dorado is known to travel in pairs.

The **king mackerel** is a long, narrow fish with a dark thin stripe along its side and spots below the stripe. The larg-est of the mackerels, it grows to 35 in/90 cm; the largest ever found measured 72 in/180 cm and weighed 100 lb/

45 kg. King mackerel usually live to be 14 years old, although some studies show them to live almost twice that long. Size determines sexual maturity and they spawn from May to September.

Tuna are found around the world between the cold northern or southern waters to the equator. The bluefin tuna, the largest of this group, can reach 180 in/455 cm and can weigh 1,500 lb/680 kg. However, the most common size is about 75 in/200 cm. Because of the quality of the meat, these fish can sell for up to $45,000 each in Japan. Tuna become sexually mature at about four or five years and live to 15 years on average. They travel in schools when young. The schools are often a mixed bunch of students determined by size rather than species.

> **FACT FILE:** *Tuna like to swim as deep as 3,000 feet/1,000 meters and can cross the Atlantic Ocean in 60 days, swimming an average speed of 45 mph/ 75 kph.*

NATIONAL EMBLEMS

NATIONAL FLAG

The national flag has three vertical stripes of equal size. The colors are green, white and red, with the white center stripe holding the coat of arms. The present flag was adopted in 1968 to update it for the Olympics being held in Mexico that year.

NATIONAL ANTHEM

The lyrics of the national anthem were written by **Francisco Gonzalez Bocanegra** and the music was composed by **Jaime Nuò**. It was declared the national anthem in 1854.

Mexicans, at the cry of battle,
prepare your swords and bridle;
and let the earth tremble at its center
at the roar of the cannon.

O Fatherland! Your forehead shall be girded
with olive garlands, by the divine archangel of peace.
For in heaven your eternal destiny
has been written by the hand of God.

But should a foreign enemy dare to profane
your land with his sole.
Think, beloved fatherland,
that heaven gave you a soldier in each son.
War, war without truce against who would attempt to
blemish the honor of the fatherland!

War, war!
The patriotic banners drench in waves of blood.

War, war!
On the mount, in the valley,
the terrifying thunder of the cannon
and the echoes nobly resound
to the cries of the Union! Liberty!

Fatherland, before your children become
unarmed beneath the yoke their necks in sway,
and your countryside be watered with blood,
on blood their feet trample.
And may your temples, palaces and towers crumble
in horrid crash and ruins remain saying:
the fatherland was made of one thousand heroes.

Fatherland, fatherland,
your children swear to exhale
their breath in your cause
if the bugle in its belligerent tone
should call upon them to struggle with bravery.

For you the olive garlands!
For them a memory of glory!
For you a laurel of victory!
For them a tomb of honor!

COAT OF ARMS

The coat of arms is designed after the legend of the Mexican people. The gods told them to find a place where an eagle, eating a snake, landed on a prickly-pear cactus. After years of wondering, the people found the site and in 1325 started building a city on the island in the  swamp where the eagle was found. The place became the center of religion, politics and commerce until it fell under the cannons of Hernando Cortez. To the Mexican people, the eagle was a symbol of war and in other pieces of art it can be found attacking a snake or a jaguar.

NATIONAL PRAYER

National prayer, or the Initial Prayers for Mexico, are the traditional devotions of the Roman Catholic Church. During an Act of Contrition (during confession) a Mexican will recite:

O my God I am heartily sorry for having offended you, and I detest all my sins because I fear the loss of heaven and the pains of hell, but most of all because they offend you my God, who are all good and deserving of all my love. I firmly resolve, with the help of your grace, to sin no more and to avoid the near occasions of sin. Amen.

NATIONAL BIRD

The national bird is a raptor, a scavenger and, sadly, now on the endangered list. To learn more about the **cara cara**, see page 41.

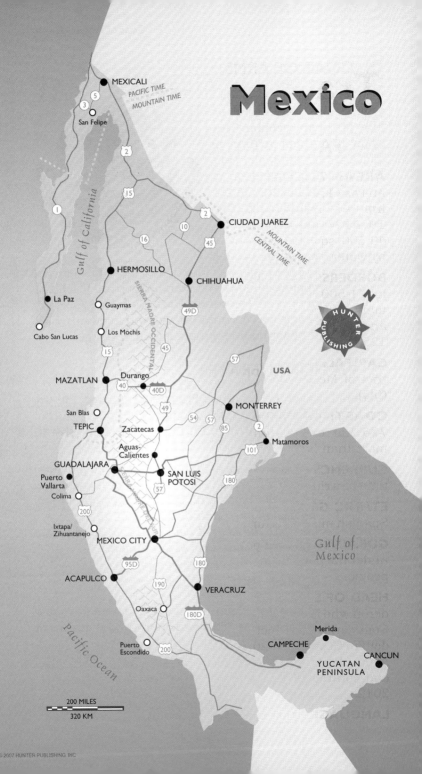

Mexico

MEXICALI

PACIFIC TIME

MOUNTAIN TIME

5

3

San Felipe

2

15

CIUDAD JUAREZ

10

2

MOUNTAIN TIME

CENTRAL TIME

45

16

1

Gulf of California

HERMOSILLO

CHIHUAHUA

La Paz

Guaymas

49D

Cabo San Lucas

Los Mochis

45

SIERRA MADRE OCCIDENTAL

57

USA

15

Durango

MAZATLAN

40

40D

49

MONTERREY

San Blas

TEPIC

Zacatecas

54

57

85

2

Matamoros

Aguas-Calientes

101

GUADALAJARA

SAN LUIS POTOSI

180

Puerto Vallarta

Colima

57

200

Ixtapa/Zihuantanejo

MEXICO CITY

95D

180

Gulf of Mexico

ACAPULCO

190

Oaxaca

180D

VERACRUZ

Merida

Pacific Ocean

Puerto Escondido

200

CAMPECHE

YUCATAN PENINSULA

CANCUN

200 MILES

320 KM

© 2007 HUNTER PUBLISHING, INC

Travel Information

FACTS AT YOUR FINGERTIPS

AREA: 742,474 sq miles/1,923,000 sq km of land, with 19,112 sq miles/49,500 sq km covered by water.

BORDERS: USA, 2,414 km/1,500 mi, Guatemala, 800 km/500 mi and Belize, 200 km/125 mi.

CAPITAL: Federal District of Mexico (Mexico City).

COAST: 450 miles/725 km of coastline, more than half of which is on the western shore.

CURRENCY: The peso, the value of which fluctuates. At time of writing, it was 10.4 pesos for US $1.

ETHNIC GROUPS: 60% mestizo (American Indian and Spanish mix), 30% American Indian, 9% white, 1% other.

GDP: US $9,600 per person, but 40% of the population is under the poverty line. There is a labor force of 40 million people.

HEAD OF STATE: The new Head of State is Felipe Calderòn who is the Head of State, Head of Government, and Commander-in-Chief of the military. He became president in September, 2006 and is a member of the National Action Party (PAN). Opposed to abortion, gay marriage and contraception, he will be in office until December, 2012.

LANGUAGES: Spanish, Mayan, Nahuatl.

Pico de Orizaba.

HIGHEST/LOWEST POINT: Pico de Orizaba, 17,500 feet/5,350 meters; Laguna Salada, at 30 feet/10 meters.

LIFE EXPECTANCY: Average is 69 for males and 75 for females.

POPULATION: 105 million (estimated), with a growth rate of 1.43% and 2.53 children per family.

RELIGION: 89% Roman Catholic, 6% protestant and 5% other religions, including Buddhism, Hinduism, Sikhism and Taoism.

RESOURCES: Petroleum, silver, copper, gold, lead, zinc, natural gas and timber.

TRANSPORTATION: 10,000 miles/16,000 km of railway; 175,000 miles/282,000 km of highway; and 1,500 miles/2,400 km of navigable rivers and coastal canals. There are 231 airports with paved runways and 1,592 without.

WHEN TO GO

Mexicans travel within their own country a lot, so be certain to have your room booked during the peak seasons like Christmas, Easter and summer vacation, from June to mid-August.

At Easter and Christmas, most Mexicans close shop and spend time with their families. During these holidays, the large hotels will serve meals, but almost everything else will be closed. During any other festival, everything remains open. This is especially true in tourist areas. Only in the smaller villages may you find things closed; if you need anything, seek out the local proprietor.

NATICONAL & RELIGIOUS HOLIDAYS

■ **January**

1st – **New Year's Day**

6th – **Dia de los Santos Reyes** is when Mexicans exchange Christmas presents. The day corresponds to the day the Three Wise Men brought Jesus gifts.

17th – **Feast Day of San Antonio de Abad** is when animals are blessed in the church.

■ **February**

5th – **Dia de la Constitución** is when the constitution was inaugurated.

24th – **Flag Day** honors the national flag.

■ **March**

Carnival is the weekend before lent, 40 days before Easter. The date changes every year. Carnival is celebrated with parades, street dancing, partying and feasting. Mazatlan is the best town on the west coast in which to enjoy this celebration.

21st – Birthday of **Benito Juarez**, a national hero and one of the early presidents.

■ **April**

Semana Santa is the week of Easter and includes Good Friday and Easter Sunday. To celebrate, Mexicans like to break eggs filled with confetti over the heads of friends and family.

■ **May**

1st – **Primero de Mayo** is equivalent to Labor Day in the US.

5th – **Cinco de Mayo** honors the battle and victory over the French at Puebla de los Angeles in 1862.

10th – **Mother's Day** is especially important in Mexico.

▓ June

1st – **Navy Day** is when coastal cities celebrate the importance of the Navy for defending the country. They have regattas and parades with decorated ships.

▓ September

The annual **State of the Union**, when the president addresses the nation, is held at the start of September; the date changes.

16th – **Independence Day** is the day Miguel Hidalgo announced the revolution against the Spanish.

▓ October

12th – **Dia de la Raza** commemorates the arrival of Columbus in America.

▓ November

1st & 2nd – **Dia de los Muertos** is when Mexicans honor the spirits of their ancestors by visiting their graves, decorating them and feasting.

20th – **Revolution Day** commemorates the Mexican Revolution of 1910.

▓ December

12th – **Dia de Nuestra Señora de Guadalupe** honors the patron saint of Mexico.

16th – **Las Posadas** starts the Christmas celebrations with a candlelight procession and commemorates the search for shelter by Joseph and Mary.

25th – **Christmas Day**

▓ SEASONAL CONSIDERATIONS

Head to the Pacific coast between November and February if you want ideal weather. If you don't mind high heat and humidity, you can go at other times. The farther north you are, the longer the "winter season" of warm days and cool nights. During this season, daytime temperatures at northern beaches hover around 70°F/21°C, while evenings are cool, sometimes as low as 50°F/10°C. The humidity is between 30 and 50% and the rains have generally stopped. However, during the summer months, humidity is often around 80%, and temperatures are quite a bit higher than in winter.

From December to March, the central coast has warm weather, with day-time temperatures in the low to mid-80s and evenings in the mid-60s to 70s F (15-21°C). Summers are oppressively hot and hurricanes threaten between June and September. This is also rainy season.

The southern coast has much less rain than the north, and the humidity is generally never below 50%. Coupled with temperatures between the mid-70s and low 90s F (21-32°C), this makes for a hot visit. The best months to visit are between December and February. The rest of the time, the high temperatures and humidity can be too much to bear.

WHAT TO TAKE

REQUIRED DOCUMENTS

Under new government regulations, by January 8, 2007, travelers going to and from the Caribbean, Mexico and Canada – plus Bermuda and Panama – will be required to have a passport to enter or re-enter the United States. On

December 31, 2007, the requirement will be extended to all land-based border crossings as well.

> **IMPORTANT:** *It is the recommendation of this author that every member of the family carry a valid passport for international travel.*

Children under 18 who are citizens of Canada or the United States may travel with a birth certificate but without a photo identification card. However, it is advisable to have a photo ID also. Children not traveling with both their legal guardians must have a notarized letter of consent from the non-traveling parent with permission for the child to cross international borders. A child too young to have received his birth certificate must have a notarized letter from the pediatrician or hospital identifying the child as belonging to the adult.

> ▶▶ **AUTHOR TIP:** *In our technological age you can scan your passport and e-mail the scan to your traveling e-mail address (i.e., Yahoo, Hotmail). This way, you always have a copy. You can do this with your postcard or e-mail address list also.*

Mexicans residing in the US may travel one way with a Mexican passport (even if it is expired) or they may present a Matricula Consular that is a Certificate of Nationality issued by the Mexican Consulate. Those using the Matricula Consular must have a photo identification card and birth certificate. If this is not possible, the Matricula Consular may be presented with a Mexican voter registration paper and a photo identification card. An American green card will not allow Mexican citizens permission to enter into Mexico, but the green card will get them back into the US.

Once in Mexico, and if staying more than 72 hours past the border zones like Tijuana, you will receive a **tourist card**. Do not lose this card as it will take a lot of complicated bureaucracy and a bit of money to get another.

There is no charge for a tourist card when it is first issued.

VISAS, PLEASE

Citizens of the following countries are not required to show a visa to enter Mexico for tourist purposes, but they must have a valid passport: Andorra, Argentina, Australia, Austria, Belgium, Bermuda, Brazil, Costa Rica, Chile, Czech Republic, Denmark, France, Finland, Germany, Great Britain, Greece, Hungary, Ireland, Iceland, Israel, Italy, Japan, Liechtenstein, Luxembourg, Monaco, Norway, New Zealand, Netherlands, Poland, Portugal, San Marino, Singapore, Slovenia, South Korea, Spain, South Africa, Switzerland, Uruguay, Venezuela and Sweden.

Citizens of the following countries are required to obtain a visa, as outlined above: Afghanistan, Albania, Angola, Armenia, Azerbaijan, Bahrain, Bangladesh, Belarus, Bosnia-Herze-govina, Cambodia, Congo, Croatia, Estonia, Georgia, Haiti, India, Iraq, Iran, Jordan, Kazakhstan, Latvia, Lebanon, Libya, Lithuania, Macedonia, Mauritania, Moldavia, Mongolia, Morocco, Niger, North Korea, Oman, Pakistan, Palestine, Qatar, Russia, Sahara Democratic Republic, Saudi Arabia, Somalia, Sri Lanka, Sudan, Syria, Tunisia, Turkmenistan, Turkey, Ukraine, United Arab Emirates, Uzbekistan, Vietnam, Yemen and Yugoslavia.

Citizens of the following countries must also apply for a visa to visit Mexico, but they need not pay the US $37 consular fee: Bolivia, Colombia, Dominican Republic, Jamaica, Nicaragua, Peru, Ecuador, Rumania, Belize, Panama, Guatemala and Malaysia.

Depending upon your reasons for traveling to Mexico, as well as your country of citizenship, you may be required to obtain a **visa**. Residents of some countries must apply for a visa to the Mexican consulate or embassy in their own countries before they arrive at the Mexican border. If there is no embassy or consulate, you must apply by mail to the immigration authorities in Mexico City (Mexican Ministry of the Interior, National Institute of Migration, Ejercito Nactional #862, Col. Los Morales/Sección Palmas, Mexico, DF, 11540). For more specific information, visit www.embamexican.com. It takes six to eight weeks to process this type of visa and only those applying for a visa may enter the Mexican consulate or embassy in their country. The cost is US $37 and must be paid in cash or money order.

People who want to retire or reside in Mexico must have a special visa. For this one-year, multiple-entry visa you must present a valid passport, application form, photos, health certificate, letter from your local police department stating that you are free of a police record, letter from the bank stating that your monthly income exceeds $2,000 plus $1,000 for each dependent. And finally, you must pay a consular fee of $136 in cash or money order. This type of visa takes three days to process and can be extended on a yearly basis for a period of five years, after which permanent residence status must be obtained.

FACT FILE: *If you make money in Mexico, you are subject to Mexican taxes and eligible for social security.*

For more information about immigration laws for retirees, contact the **Mexican Ministry of the Interior**, National Institute of Migration, Ejercito Nactional #862, Col. Los Morales/Sección Palmas, Mexico, DF, 11540. Specific information about becoming a Mexican resident is offered at www.embamexican.com/consular/resident.html.

Canadian and American journalists traveling in Mexico for a special event (or to write a book like this) must get an FM-3 migratory form from the nearest consular office in their country. This document allows the journalist to remain in Mexico for 90 days and to make multiple entries.

Working in Mexico requires a special visa. Workers may fill positions in the country that cannot be filled first by Mexicans. Companies big enough to require a foreign president, treasurer, general manager, and so on, must comply with the 90% Mexican employee to 10% foreign employee ratio. Professionals such as doctors, lawyers and engineers may receive immigrant status if they have their degrees and a special license to practice in Mexico. Investors must have 26,000 times the current daily minimum wage (between 46 and 49 pesos) to invest in Mexico before opening a company. At today's exchange rate, that's US $120,000 to US $128,000, but the peso value fluctuates regularly. This money must be in the Mexican Development Bank guaranteeing that investment will be made within a specific time period. This time period is determined by the National Institute of Migration.

TRAVELING WITH PETS

You can bring pets into Mexico as long as you have a certificate from a veterinarian, issued within the last seven days, stating the animal is free of communicable diseases. You also need a rabies vaccination certificate showing that the pet was vaccinated at least one month and less than one year before crossing the border. It is advisable to have pet travel insurance. Taking any exotic or endangered pet like a macaw into Mexico is not permitted and the animal could be confiscated at the border.

Returning to the US with a traveling pet, you must have a vet's certificate saying the pet had a rabies shot within the preceding three years.

PACKING LIST

Binoculars are a must if you are a birder. There is an abundance of exotic and migratory birds that are well worth scouting out. Binoculars are also fun to use on the beach to watch boats (and those on the boats) as they pass by. I even use mine on bus trips to look at distant hills and volcanoes.

Shorts and **t-shirts** are great. Everyone wears shorts, but a skirt or pants are acceptable too. Keep your clothing loose and comfortable – let the heat determine your attire, but keep in mind that revealing outfits are not acceptable. If you are a touch stodgy (like me) be prepared to be shocked by some of your fellow tourists as you wander the beach.

If going during the rainy season, May to September, pack some type of **rain protection**. **Sandals** are good at the beach, but **running shoes** or light **hiking boots** are needed for jungle walks, playing golf or touring the museums.

You will need at least one **bathing suit** and two would be better. A beach towel or grass mat is good for lying on the sand. Mats can be purchased along the beaches for less than $5.

Cameras are a great way to record memories. Bring one that you are familiar with so that you don't make mistakes on critical images. Humidity is high, so keeping your camera dry is an issue. I use a foam-padded carrying bag. Putting cameras in plastic bags is not advisable as the moisture condenses inside the bag. Non-expired film, camera batteries and flashes are readily available. Because there is so much intense sunlight, a slow-speed film is recommended (ASA 50 to 100). A flash should be used when photographing people during the day so that the harsh shadows are eliminated.

Money belts are necessary if you want to carry money with you rather than using an ATM each time you need cash. They are also good to hold credit, bank cards, and your passport. The belts should be of natural fiber and worn at the midriff. Always have a stash of emergency money somewhere in the event that you are robbed and lose your bank card and credit card in the process.

Daypacks are far more convenient to carry than handbags or beach bags. They are also harder to pickpocket or snatch. In cities, on buses or crowded places like markets, wear your daypack at the front, with the waist strap done up. That way, your hands can rest on the bag while you walk. In this position, it is almost impossible for pickpockets to access the pack. Keep only the amount of money you need for the day in your daypack and put the rest somewhere secure, like in your hotel safe or your hidden money belt.

Tennis players should bring their own rackets because they, like other sports gear, are quite personal.

Golf clubs are also personal and should be brought with you. However, for those able to adapt to any clubs, rentals are most convenient.

Diving gear like wet suits and face masks can be brought from home or rented from dive shops. You will need your PADI diving certification ticket. The tour operators check this certificate every time you go out. You should also check their qualifications before heading into the depths.

Diving is a popular pastime.

Snorkeling mask and **flippers** can be carried with you from home or rented in Mexico. If going to only one resort, bringing your gear is not a problem but if traveling around, you may find it easier to rent.

Surf boards can be taken as a piece of luggage on the plane. Hardcore surfers should definitely bring their own board, but if you are a beginner, you can get away with renting.

Camping equipment should be brought with you if you are traveling around from beach to beach, sleeping in the campgrounds. Sleeping on secluded beaches is not recommended, although I know people do it. You will need a tent with mosquito netting, sleeping pad and a light cover. Cooking stoves should be able to use gasoline rather than white gas because of the availability of these fuels. The extent of your camping will determine what you will bring with you.

Maps are essential. The best I have found is published by International Travel Maps and Books, 530 West Broadway, Vancouver, BC, ☎ 604-879-3621, www.itmb.com, and sells for less than $20. Their maps, Mexican Pacific Coast and Mexico Northwest, are easy to read, but do not have every village and pueblo included.

It seems to me that a map is really hard to follow if you don't have a **compass**. They are not heavy and you need not buy one that can do triangulation measurements. A simple one will do.

An **umbrella** is good if you plan on doing any walking. It keeps off the sun or rain. These can be purchased in Mexico for about the same price or a little less than those at home.

Your **first aid kit** should include things like mole-skin, Advil, tenser bandage, antihistamines, topical antibiotic cream and Band-Aids. All prescription medications and things like batteries for hearing aides or extra eyeglasses should be carried with you. A band that attaches to your glasses and goes around your head to keep glasses from falling off is a good idea if you are even a little bit active.

Reading material is available in English at the magazine stands or bookstores. In addition, many hotels have book-trading services. But for the most part, you need to bring the really good books with you. Leaving them behind when you return home is a good idea. There are some places, like the Mazatlan Reading Library, Sixto Osuna #115, MazLibrary@mexconnect.com, where you can borrow books and leave any that you have already read.

Sunglasses and **sun hat** should be brought and worn all the time you are in the sun because the intense ultraviolet rays can damage your eyes. If you forget to bring these, they are readily available in all the markets.

FACT FILE: *Paul Theroux, author of Patagonia Express and other travel books, has problems with his eyes due to the damage caused by the ultraviolet rays. He often kayaked without sunglasses.*

Sunscreen is necessary. Do not let yourself become cancer red because you don't like chemicals. If spending time in the jungle, you should bring **insect repellent**.

HEALTH CONCERNS

Geneary health should be kept at optimum level when traveling. Make certain you have rest, lots of clean water and a well-balanced diet that is supplemented with vitamins. This is not difficult to do. Salt intake is important in the heat to help prevent dehydration. Carry some powdered electrolytes in case you do become dehydrated, especially if you are planning some off-the-beach trips.

Bring with you anything you may need in the way of prescriptions, glasses, orthopedics, dental care and batteries for hearing aids. Things like vitamins, bandages, antihistamines and topical creams are readily available.

MEDICAL INSURANCE

Mexico now has almost the same quality medical services as the rest of North America and Europe, but it is still advisable to travel with medical insurance. The cost is far less than any medical bill would be and many policies include ticket cancellation insurance and coverage against theft.

In the event of a serious illness or accident, you will want to get to your own country fast. Without insurance, the cost could be prohibitive.

Good insurance includes emergency evacuation, repatriation, emergency reunion, trip interruption, lost baggage, accidental death and trip cancellation.

For US citizens, the following table gives you an idea of what it will cost for $50,000 coverage with a $100 deductible. For each additional month but under a year, multiply the monthly premium cost by the number of months you will be staying. Those staying longer than three months are usually eligible for a 10% discount. Groups traveling together are often offered a lower rate.

INSURANCE COST GUIDELINES		
Individual	**15-Day Premium**	**30-Day Premium**
Age 18-29	$24	$48
Age 30-39	$31	$62
Age 40-49	$47	$94
Age 50-59	$67	$134
Age 60-64	$79	$158
Age 65-69	$90	$180
Age 70-79	$122	$244
Age 80+	$212	$424

It is recommended that anyone traveling for longer than a month take out insurance of up to a million dollars.

I worked with Patricia Romero Hamrick from **International Insurance-Seguros**, 1047 W. Madero Mesa, AZ 85210-7635, ☎ 480-345-0191, www.seguros-insurance. net. I found her helpful and quick to answer any questions. She also works through **Global Travel Insurance**, ☎ 800-232-9415, www.globalmedicalplans.com. The best thing about this company's insurance is that it covers emergency evacuation and reunion, which means a loved-one can be brought to your bedside in the event that you are in hospital away from home for a long time. Moderate expenses for this loved-one are included. Global Travel also carries a Hazardous Sports Rider for those partaking in sports such as mountain biking or rock climbing. This is especially important for the serious sportster.

WATER

Tap water, called purified water, is considered safe to drink in luxury hotels. If you feel uncomfortable with this, bottled water is available throughout the country. It comes in sizes from half a liter (pint) to four liters (one gallon). When there is no sign, water is considered drinkable. If there is a W1 or W2 sign, it means the water is untreated and not drinkable.

Use your common sense to avoid illness. Eat at places where locals are eating. If they remain healthy, you should too. An empty restaurant usually means a bad stomach. If the sanitation looks dubious, don't eat the salad; have some hot boiled soup instead.

If traveling where creek/lake water must be consumed, I suggest using a chemical such as iodine for purification. There is also a tablet available that has a silver (as opposed to an iodine) base that is far more palatable than the iodine. Chlorine bleach can also be used as a purifier, but it is the least effective of chemicals.

Mechanical filters take a long time to process the water and they do not filter out all organisms that could cause problems. They are also much heavier to carry than chemicals.

COMMON AILMENTS

Should you get a mild case of **diarrhea**, take a day of rest, drink plenty of mineral water and consume no alcohol. This common condition, often caused by the change in diet, usually clears up quickly. Mineral water can be supplemented with yogurt tablets. Imodium can be taken if you must travel and have a bad case of the trots. However, it is not recommended except in very dire emergencies because holding in the cause of your problems will allow them to multiply and make you even sicker, sometimes even causing scaring of the intestinal tissue.

FEVERS & WORSE

According to the World Health Organization, contacting **malaria** is a possibility all year at elevations below 3,000 ft/950 meters anywhere from Guaymas in the north all the way south to the Guatemala bordcr in the south. The states of Sonora and Sinaloa are free of malaria except for the months between May and October, during rainy season.

People staying at major resorts need not use a prophylactic against malaria, but should use mosquito repellent after sunset or if going into the jungle. Anyone traveling around the country – especially those staying in lower-priced hotels – will need to use a prophylactic. Chloroquine is the prophylactic of choice. It should be taken for one week before entering the country, once a week while there, and for four weeks after returning home.

In the event that you develop a fever for no explicable reason like a cold or flu, especially if you are in mosquito country or have been bitten, you should see a doctor as soon as possible. The possibility of malaria should be considered for up to three months after leaving an infected area.

PROTECTION IS BEST

Keep exposed skin covered early in the morning or at dusk when the mosquitoes are most active. Using repellent laced with deet is also recommended. Although traces of deet have been found in the livers of users, this problem is still better than malaria. Use a sleeping net in infected areas.

Dengue fever and **dengue hemorrhagic fever** are caused by four related, but distinctly different, viruses that are spread by daytime-biting mosquitoes. Infection from one of the viruses does not produce immunity to the other three. Dengue cannot be transmitted from person to person.

Symptoms of dengue are high fever, headache, backache, joint pain, nausea, vomiting, eye pain and rash. There is no treatment except to take painkillers with acetaminophen in them rather than ASA (acetylsalicylic acid decreases your blood's clotting abilities, thus increasing the possibility of hemorrhage). Drink plenty of fluids and rest. If dengue hemorrhagic fever is contacted, fluid replacement therapy administered by a medical practitioner may be necessary. The illness lasts about 10 days and total recovery takes between two and four weeks.

Dengue is now on the rise worldwide. In 1960s, the WHO stated that there were about 30,000 cases worldwide. By 1995, this number increased to 592,000, with 240,000 cases in Mexico. Today, with the increase in urbanization and decrease in eradication programs, the WHO believes there are 20 million cases worldwide. This means that mosquito bites are potentially dangerous in the tropics. For more information, visit the website of the World Resource Institute at www.wri.org/wr-98-99/dengue.htm.

Yellow fever is present in all the jungles of Central America. Though inoculation is not required for entrance to Mexico, it may be required for re-entry to your own country. Inoculation, good for 10 years, is recommended if you want to avoid a lengthy stay in quarantine. Children must also have a certificate of inoculation, but it is not recommended to inoculate children who are less than one year of age.

Routine inoculations common in your home country should be up to date. Besides these, **immune globulin** is recommended against viral hepatitis; the shots are good for about six months. If you have had viral hepatitis, you are already immune. Inoculation against **typhoid fever** is highly recommended and is good for 10 years.

BUGS

Worms and **parasites** can be a problem anywhere in the tropics. To name and describe them all would be impossible. Keep your feet free of cuts or open sores so that worm eggs or parasites cannot enter. Use sandals in showers where cleanliness is a question. Wear closed shoes, such as runners or hiking boots, in the jungle.

The **bot fly** and the **New World screw worm** are insects that cause a boil-like sore after the larvae (maggot) has started to grow in its host (you). Botflies transport their eggs by way of the mosquito and the screw worm in the fly stage drops its eggs near an open sore or on mucus membranes. Once the egg is in its host, it hatches and lives under the skin. However, the fly must have air. If you have a red, puss-filled swelling that is larger than a mosquito bite, look closely. If you see a small hole in the swollen area cover it with petroleum jelly to prevent the fly from breathing. Without air, it dies. It takes four to eight days for the botfly larvae to hatch and five to 12 weeks for the screw worm.

Chagas, also known as the kissing bug, exists in Latin America and infection can become either chronic or acute. The parasite enters the blood stream when the oval-shaped insect inserts its proboscis into your skin. As it sucks your blood, its excretion is forced out and into the opening it has formed in your body. It is the excretion that carries the larvae of the parasite.

Once planted, the larvae migrates to the heart, brain, liver and spleen, where it nests and forms cysts. If you wake up one morning after sleeping under a thatched roof and you have a purplish lump somewhere on exposed skin, you may have been bitten. If fever, shortness of breath, vomiting or convulsions occur, see a doctor immediately. Mention your suspicions.

JELLYFISH STINGS

These are a possibility for anyone who enters the water. There are often flags along the beach indicating that jellyfish are present and what their parameters are. Some stings can leave a welt for weeks, but most last only a few hours. When a jellyfish stings you, it is actually the nematocysts attached to the tentacles that touch your skin and release a toxin. This is what burns. If you do get stung, douse the area with vinegar and cover with ice to relieve the pain. A product available in the US called "After Sting Gel," which sells for $4, can be used for jellyfish and bee stings. For more information on jellyfish, see www.diversalertnetwork.com.

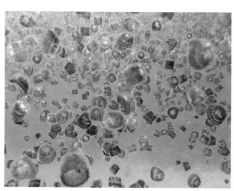

A brood of jellyfish off Mexico's coast.

TREATMENT OPTIONS

If you become sick, contact your own consulate for the names of doctors or medical clinics. The consulates can usually recommend doctors who have been trained in your country of origin.

An alternative is to contact the **IAMAT** (International Association for Medical Assistance to Travelers) clinics. The doctors speak English or French and Spanish (in Mexico) and charge between $55 for an office visit to $95 for an emergency call-out at night or on Sundays.

The information reported in this section is taken from either the IAMAT's or the World Health Organization's publications. You can become a member of IAMAT and/or send a donation to them at 417 Center Street, Lewiston, NY 14092, ☎ 716-754-4883, or 40 Regal Road, Guelph, Ontario, Canada, N1H 7L5, ☎ 519-836-0102, www.sentex.net/~iamat.com. Their services are invaluable. Some of the money they raise goes toward a scholarship program that assists doctors in developing countries obtain medical training in more advanced parts of the world. They also sell, at cost, a portable mosquito net that weighs about five lbs/two kilos.

SAFE INDEED

IAMAT was started when Vincenzo Marcolongo, a graduate of medicine from McGill University, was working in Rome in 1960 and saw an ill Canadian who had previously seen a local doctor. He had been given a drug that was banned in North America because it destroyed white blood cells. Blood transfusions and antibiotics saved the patient's life. Realizing the problems of language and culture for foreign visitors, Dr. Marcolongo started a worldwide list of North American- and European-trained doctors that could be available for travelers. Over 200,000 contributing members now receive the directory containing 850 doctors working in 125 countries.

IAMAT CLINICS

Remember, no area code is needed when making a local call.

■ Hermosillo, Sonora

Clinica de Praga #1 Altos, Juarez y Jalisco, ☎ 662-213-2280

■ Mazatlan

Clinica Mazatlan, Zaragoza #609, ☎ 669-981-2917 or 669-985-1923

Alternative medicines are popular and as North Americans get more and more into natural health, herbal treatment for minor ailments may be a priority. There are some locals who learned from their ancestors the art of medicine using jungle plants and they are willing to treat or share information with visitors. However, for more serious ailments like a burst appendix or a broken leg, I recommend the use of traditional scientific medicine that uses strong drugs or surgery.

For official government updates on outbreaks, advisories and more, visit the **Centers for Disease Control & Prevention** run by the US Health Department at www.cdc.gov.

Medic Alert is an emergency response service that has been in business since 1956. Members get a bracelet that has their membership number on the back. If you have a medical condition that could result in your hospitalization while you are in an unconscious state, the medical staff contacts the 24-hour service at Medic Alert, providing your membership number. Medic Alert relays your medical conditions and any necessary precautions that must be taken. They also call your family. Medic Alert can be contacted at ☎ 888-633-4298 in the US or 209-668-3333, from elsewhere, www.medicalert.org.

Critical Air Ambulance, ☎ 800-247-8326 in the US or 800-010-0268 in Mexico. This is a team of medical experts who transport patients with multiple injuries, cardiac failure, severe head injuries, cerebral bleeds, and so forth, to the nearest fully equipped hospital in the United States. If your medical insurance handles air evacuation then they may well use this company. If not, keep the number handy in case you or a member of your group needs to get home quickly. The cost would be around US $10,000.

Sky Med, ☎ 800-475-9633 in US and Canada, 866-805-9624 in Mexico, www.skymed.com, is another company that will take you home in the event of an emergency. They go one step farther by insuring that your vehicle and all belongings also get home. They will allow a companion to travel at your bedside during the trip. Sky Med will take Canadians to a Canadian hospital if time permits, rather than an American one. This is not an expensive insurance, especially for anyone doing extreme sports where chance of accident is high. An evacuation could cost up to $30,000 from Mazatlan to Chicago (for example), so some type of insurance is advisable.

MONEY MATTERS

Mexico is a good deal even though prices have risen with the signing of the North American Free Trade Agreement. You can expect to pay about half of what you would in the United States for a comparable vacation. All-inclusive packages are often almost as cheap as airfare alone and those on a strict budget can almost always find a clean hotel for about $20 a night. The cost of an average vacation in a three-star hotel with restaurant food and at

BANKS OPERATING IN MEXICO	
A visit to the bank websites will enable you to monitor the exchange rate for the day.	
Banamex/Citibank	www.banamex.com
Banco de Mexico	www.banxico.org.mx
Bancrecer	www.bancrecer.com.mx
Bancomext	www.bancomext.com
Cancomer	www.bancomer.com.mx
Banorte	www.banorte.com
Bital	www.bital.com.mx
Santander	www.santander.com.mx

least one activity a day will run about $100 per person, per day. If sharing a room, the cost drops to half for every additional person.

▩ BANKING/EXCHANGE

The local currency is the **peso** and it is indicated by the $ sign. Each peso is divided into 100 **centavos**. Coins come in denominations of 10, 20 and 50 centavos and one, two, five, 10 and 20 pesos. Notes come in the two, five, 10, 20, 50, 100 and 200 peso denominations. At time of writing, the exchange rate was about 10 pesos to US $1 and 13 pesos to one Euro.

Foreign money can be exchanged at the banks or Casas des Cambios. Banks are open 9 am-1:30 pm, Monday to Friday, and a few banks are open on Saturday afternoons. Casas are open later in the day, but seldom on Sundays. The exchange rate for cash is always higher than that for traveler's checks.

Traveler's checks issued by Visa, American Express or Thomas Cook are accepted throughout the country. The preferred currency is the American dollar.

There are over 9,000 ATMs in Mexico and, although there are plenty, finding one can sometimes be tricky as they are usually not open to the street. Occasionally, you will have to ask a local. Grocery stores are a good place to access these machines because, as a foreigner, you have the protection of a crowd and a gun-wielding guard. You can usually withdraw US/CAN $500 per day from your account (as long as the cash is in there to begin with), more than enough for your daily travels.

▩ CREDIT CARDS

Credit Cards are acceptable anywhere except at the tiniest food stall or market merchant. The most common are **Visa**, **MasterCard**, **Diner's Club Card** and **American Express**.

If you need money wired from home, contact **Money Gram**, www.moneygram.com, or **Western Union**, www.

westernunion.com. Visit their websites to obtain local office numbers.

PLANNING EXPENSES

If you make all your own arrangements, your cheapest day could run about $50 per person. This would include a basic room with a fan, two meals in the market or one of the smaller restaurants and the entrance fee to one attraction, like a museum. Your main entertainment would be sunning on the beach and reading a book which you brought with you. Should you want to do more – whale watch, scuba dive or play golf – the price goes up substantially. A better hotel will cost another $50, and drinks with dinner raise the price quite a bit.

To go first class – enjoy a piña colada at your hotel while watching the sun set over the Pacific and rent a car – will run between $250 and $500 per day. Most people budget for somewhere between the two extremes. There are, of course, a few places that offer even more than first class; prices at such resorts run around $1,000 a day.

HOTEL PRICE SCALES

For each hotel reviewed in this book, I give a price range rather than a fixed rate. The price for a single and double room is the same unless otherwise stated. Use these rates as a guideline only; always call and verify current prices.

HOTEL PRICE SCALE
Price for a room given in US $.
$. . . . . .Up to $20
$$. . . . . $21-$50
$$$. . . . . $51-$100
$$$$ . . . . $101-$150
$$$$$ . . . . $151-$200

For each establishment, I give my personal impression, followed by a brief review. My impressions may have been influenced by whom I saw and how they treated me. Once you have used the book for a while, you will have an idea as to what events and experiences interest me and what level of service I expect.

■ TAXES & TIPPING

There is a 15% **Value Added Tax** (VAT) on everything for sale, except food purchased at a grocery store and medicines. Hotels have a 12% tax and you may also be charged 10% service charge over the quoted price for the room. Ask before booking.

Tipping is expected in restaurants and hotels. However, if a service charge is added to the bill, I fail to see why a tip would be expected; I don't tip. Taxi drivers appreciate a tip, although it isn't necessary. The average tip is between 10% and 15%, depending on the service.

DANGERS & ANNOYANCES

Some houses in Mexico are secured by high concrete walls that have glass shards or razor-wire cemented along the top and steel bars on the windows. Inside, there are either vicious guard dogs or security guards armed with machine guns. Banks, too, have armed guards, as do some of the high-end restaurants.

This high security is not an environment that nurtures a trusting personality. Instead, it produces a "get him before he gets me" attitude, which results in many rip-offs for the unsuspecting visitor. To help prevent this, always ask the price, especially if the item you want is not on the menu or if the taxi you are using has to wait while you check out of a room. If you are not comfortable with this kind of clarification, then you may want to book into an all-inclusive package and never venture into the streets. If this also is not what you want, then Mexico may not be for you.

Even with all my experience traveling in Latin American countries, I still get royally annoyed when I get taken. To avoid this, always clarify.

SCAM ALERT – GETTING A CHARGE

The latest scam is at the airports, particularly Puerto Vallarta and Acapulco. The workers at the security desks are now confiscating batteries, but only those still in packages. They tell the traveler that it is illegal to carry them on board. In fact, they are selling the batteries in the markets to supplement their incomes. You can take packaged batteries onto a plane.

AIRPORT SECURITY

Since 9-11, airport security has increased. Cameras and laptop computers are checked for explosives. People are asked to remove their shoes. I have even seen security guards demand that metal earrings be removed.

However, there are some things that most people would never think of. For an example, the explosive powders from firecrackers can set off alarms, as can the residue of explosives from those who have been at firing ranges or those who set off explosives for avalanche control. It is illegal to transport firecrackers and, if caught with them, you will be subject to a $25,000 fine and/or up to five years in prison. Fertilizer on the shoes of golfers and nitroglycerin for heart patients can also set off alarms. The most recent alarming substance is the glycerin in some hand lotions.

Doing your part in avoiding these substances before going to the airport will speed up your trip through the security monitors.

For those with a common last name, especially one like Garcia or Martinez, be aware that you may be stopped at American immigration for questioning. The interrogations usually last no longer than 10 or 15 minutes, but they are irritating. Keep your humor and matters will be dealt with much quicker.

If you are a frequent flier you should get a letter from Customs declaring that you are not "the Garcia" or "Martinez" who has a criminal record or direct links to Osama.

COMMON-SENSE PRECAUTIONS

Every country in the world has robbers and petty thieves, whether you are in the polite society of Japan or the northern wilds of Canada. If you hang out in very poor sections of a city where you are unknown, if you are staggering drunk in a back alley, if you trust a stranger to hold your cash while you run to the washroom, you are going to have a sad tale to tell.

When out, be aware of what is around you. If it seems like you are being followed, go into a store or knock on someone's door. Make certain that expensive items like your camera or Rolex watch are out of sight.

Be inside at night and take a taxi back to your hotel if you have been out late. Don't be drunk in public. A drunk is a great target. Don't get mixed up in the dope trade. Save booze and dope for home. If you do get into trouble at home, you know the rules, you have friends to help and the prisons are far more comfortable than they are in Mexico.

Women should walk with confidence. If you appear frightened or lost, you are a target. Don't walk alone in non-populated places like jungles or secluded beaches. In the event that you are grabbed or accosted in any way, create a scene. Holler, scream, kick and fight with all your might. However, if you are approached by someone with a weapon, let them have it all. Being dead or seriously maimed isn't worth any possession you have, including your virginity.

TOILETS

Be aware that the sewer systems in Mexico are not like those in the United States. Except for in the newer, up-market hotels, used toilet paper should be placed in a basket beside the toilet, rather than in it. It is a huge problem when those unaccustomed to this method of disposal refuse to follow the rules. Please be sensitive to the needs of the Mexican Public Service Department and put your paper in the basket.

MEASUREMENTS

Mexico is metric, distance is given in kilometers, gas is sold in liters, and the temperature is read in Celsius (although, to accommodate the North American tourist, it is often quoted in Fahrenheit).

GENERAL MEASUREMENTS

1 kilometer	=	.6124 miles
1 mile	=	1.6093 kilometers
1 foot	=	.304 meters
1 inch	=	2.54 centimeters
1 square mile	=	2.59 square kilometers
1 pound	=	.4536 kilograms
1 ounce	=	28.35 grams
1 imperial gallon	=	4.5459 liters
1 US gallon	=	3.7854 liters
1 quart	=	.94635 liters

TEMPERATURE

For Fahrenheit: Multiply Centigrade figure by 1.8 and add 32.

For Centigrade: Subtract 32 from Fahrenheit figure and divide by 1.8.

Centigrade		Fahrenheit
40°	=	104°
35°	=	95°
30°	=	86°
25°	=	77°
20°	=	64°
15°	=	59°
10°	=	50°

TOURIST ASSISTANCE

POLICE & OTHER AGENCIES

Mexico has almost more types of police than it has beaches. There are the Federal Police and the Federal Traffic Police. The **Federal Police** have no jurisdiction over immigration documents or other tourist-type matters. If you are stopped and asked to show documents by these people, tell them to come to your hotel. Once there, have the manager call your consulate. Because of low wages, these police have a reputation of being corrupt.

The **Tourist Police**, on the other hand, patrol areas where tourists gather. To my knowledge, they are fairly good, and I never felt threatened or unsafe when dealing with them. If you are robbed or harmed in any way, report all instances to the Tourist Police (numbers are given at the start of each town section in this book).

Green Angels (Angeles Verdes) is Mexico's national road emergency service that is in place to help motorists on major highways. They have a fleet of 300 trucks that patrol fixed sections of major highways twice a day. Drivers

Green Angels truck.

speak both English and Spanish, can help with mechanical problems, have first aid, radio-telephone communications and can tow a broken-down vehicle into a garage. Although this is a free service, a tip is always appreciated. They can be reached at ☎ 800-903-9200.

The **Consumer Protection Service**, known as the Secreteria y Fomento Turistico (SEFOTUR), is in place for complaints about businesses in Mexico. They are located in all major centers. If you have problems with a merchant, report it to this agency.

COMMUNICATIONS

▓ TELEPHONE

Most public phones require a calling card. **Ladatel cards** are sold in 20 or 50 peso denominations and are available at stores, restaurants and automated machines at the airport and bus station.

To make international calls, you must dial the international access code (98), then dial the country code (1 for the US and Canada, 44 for England), the area code and the local number. To reach Mexico from overseas, you must use the country code (52), then the city code and the number you wish to reach.

Some common city codes are: Acapulco, 744; Guadalajara, 33; Oaxaca, 951; Puerto Vallarta, 322. Codes for cities not listed here are provided at www.telmex.com. There you can type in the name of the town and get the area code. If you are placing a city-to-city call, dial 01 (for long distance), the city code and then the number. No city code is needed when making a local call.

The following numbers are used throughout Mexico.

24-hour Tourist Assistance, ☎ 800-9-0392

Emergency Assistance, ☎ 060

Operator-assisted international calls, ☎ 090

Operator-assisted national long distance, ☎ 020

Automatic national long distance, ☎ 01

Automatic long distance to Canada and the US, ☎ 001

Information, ☎ 040

To call a toll-free number from Mexico, dial, 01-8XX (numbers are usually 800, 888, 877, etc.) then the seven digits. You may find the following numbers useful.

Sprint, ☎ 01-800-877-8000

AT&T, ☎ 01-800-288-2872 or 01-800-112-2020 for Spanish.

Teleglobe Canada, ☎ 01-800-123-0200

You can also become a customer of companies like **World Wide Callback**, www.worldwidecallback.com, where you call a number that has been given to you by Callback from anywhere in the world. Once you hear the ring sound, you hang up and they call you back. From there you place your international calls. You are charged to a credit card at American rates. This system must be set up before you travel.

MAIL

It is easy and safe to send and receive mail. It takes from five to seven days for a letter/postcard to reach the United States from anywhere in Mexico. The cost for a letter is about 40¢ for up to 20 grams. Parcels don't have to be inspected before being sent out of the country, so they can be wrapped before taking them to the post office. Insurance is highly recommended for parcels.

You can receive mail at the **post restante** in any town. You will need your passport for identification to pick up your mail.

International courier services are also available: **Federal Express**, ☎ 5-228-9904 (in Mexico) or 800-900-1100, www.fedex.com; **Airborne Express**, ☎ 5-203-6811; **Aeroflash**, ☎ 5-627-3030; **DHL**, ☎ 5-345-7000, www.dhl.com; **UPS**, ☎ 5-228-7900 or 800-902-9200, www.ups.com.

MEXICAN NEWSPAPERS

English-language newspapers published for tourists are mentioned under the specific cities where they are published.

- ▓ *Reforma*, www.reforma.com, is in Spanish and covers national and international news. You must subscribe to the paper before you can read anything but the headlines.

- ▓ *El Financiero*, www.elfinanciero.com.mx, gives a summary of the financial status of Mexican economics.

- ▓ *La Jornada*, www.jornada.unam.mx, seems to be a left-wing Spanish publication.

- ▓ *Excelsior*, www.excelsior.com.mx, is an on-line magazine that you must subscribe to. You can subscribe to only the sections that are of interest to you, be they TV information, articles or tidbits.

- *El Universal*, www.eluniversal.com.mx, is a mainline newspaper with everything from headlines to horoscopes.

- *Milenio*, www.milenio.com/mexico, has national and international news, plus a good general interest section.

- *El Economista*, www.economista.com.mx, leans more toward finance than news and covers international finance too.

- *Cronica*, www.cronica.com.mx, offers general news daily.

- *El Norte*, www.elnorte.com, has full coverage daily.

- *Proceso*, www.proceso.com.mx, also has full coverage daily.

- *Expansion*, www.expansion.com.mx, makes American news a top priority.

INTERNET

The Internet is the best way to communicate; the country has over 3.5 million users. Internet cafés are almost as common as shoeshine boys. Prices are $1-2 an hour – the rate seems dependent on whether there is air conditioning in the café or not.

CULTURE SHOCK

PUBLIC AFFECTION

Once away from the beach resorts, you will find that Mexico is still a conservative country. Physical affection in public is not common. Holding hands seems to be okay, but passionate kissing, especially by same-sex couples, is still not acceptable. Mexico is a Catholic country where most people still follow the laws of the church. However, there is one nude beach at Zipolete, south of Acapulco, that the locals tolerate.

GAY & LESBIAN TRAVEL

There are numerous gay- and-lesbian-friendly bars and hotels along the coast. Cancún even held a gay festival. Although the possibility of finding a same-sex relationship with a Mexican exists, you must be careful not to think that because a Mexican has sex with you that she or he is gay. Some Mexicans look at having same-gender sex as entertainment, not a way of life.

The magazine **Ser Gay** is a good source of information for those who read Spanish. It can be found online at www.sergay.com.mx.

SPECIAL NEEDS TRAVELERS

Special needs persons are now considered in the tourist areas of Mexico and some hotels have wheelchair accessibility. The streets are still pretty shoddy in places, but taxis are plentiful. Taking a small wheelchair from a hotel to a restaurant that is on street level would be possible. Blind or deaf people should have an assistant.

FOOD

Mexican food needs no explaining to most people in North America and Europe because those countries have as many Mexican restaurants as they have hamburger and pizza joints. Mexican food is usually made up of onions, tomatoes, rice, beans, corn, eggs, cheese and *pollo* (chicken). These foods are accompanied by some kind of corn tortilla.

© 2006 About, Inc
Fruit market.

However, with the proliferation of tourism, today you can get any kind of food in Mexico, from Chinese to Japanese to Bavarian and Thai. Along the coast, of course, seafood or fish is the most popular meal. Be certain to try some ceviche, a raw fish or sea food pickled in lime juice, or *pescado* Veracruz, a fish smothered in fresh tomato and onion sauce.

Because you are in the tropics, seasonal fruits are abundant. Try guanabana, whose slimy white interior is succulent beyond belief. Taste some guava, especially if your stomach is a bit queasy as it is supposed to slow down peristaltic action in the gut. Try the mango; when fresh there is nothing like it. Banana *con leche* (banana with milk) or fresh-squeezed orange or grapefruit juice will always refresh you when you are hot or tired. Other fruits to try are avocados, grapes, papayas (larger than those found in North America), peaches, fresh-picked peanuts, pears, pineapples, strawberries, watermelons and prickly pears.

Guanabana.

FAVORITE DISHES

An **enchilada** is a tortilla stuffed with ground meat, beans and cheeses. A **tostada** is the same thing, only the tortilla is toasted and left flat on the plate.

Guacamole is made with avocado that is mashed and mixed with onion, tomato and lime juice. It is often served as an appetizer or included as one of the sauces for your meal.

FACT FILE: *Avocado is one of the few vegetables that has a lot of calories.*

Mole de pollo or **mole poblano** is considered the national dish. It consists of *mole*, a tasty brown sauce, that is cooked with either chicken or turkey. However, the *mole* sauce can be served in many ways, including as a dark thick soup. The word "mole" comes from the Aztec word meaning "sauce." When you are offered a red mole with your chicken, you should ask how spicy it is. Chances are, it has a lot of red chilies. A brown mole will have a chocolate base and be less spicy.

Chilmole is occasionally called *relleno-negro*. It is made using a sauce that incorporates orange juice, chiles, cloves, allspice, black peppers, oregano, cumin and garlic. This is cooked with either chicken or turkey.

FACT FILE: *Prior to the arrival of the Spanish, the locals made tamales for the gods, as well as for themselves. Some were made in special designs like spirals, while others were huge, weighing up to a hundred pounds.*

Tamales are a feast dish that take hours to make and only minutes to devour. They are made with a corn flour paste filled with things like meat, chiles, fish, frogs, beans, turkey, squash seeds or any combination of these foods. Most are rolled into banana leaves and steamed or roasted.

CHEF'S SECRET

Should you decide to make your own tamales once you are back at home, the one secret I can pass on to you is that a tamale, no matter how much care is taken in the making, will not turn out unless the cook has music blaring in the background.

Quesadillas are made with wheat-flour tortillas and are the same as *tostadas*, except these have tons of melted cheese on top.

Frijoles refritos, or re-fried beans. In Mexico, it matters not if you are having breakfast, snack, meal of the day or beer – *frijoles* will appear. Served with sour cream, they are delicious and an excellent source of protein.

For a good glossary of Mexican foods, as well as recipes and interesting historical tidbits, go to the TexMex website at www.texmextogo.com.

BOOKING A ROOM

Many people book their accommodations over the Internet. This is okay, but be aware that not everything on the Web is true. Photos probably show only the best side of an establishment, and lighting plays a big part in making something look far more attractive than it is. You will not see the cockroaches in the corners or hear the bus terminal next door. Rates quoted may be off-season, with no indication of what in-season rates are, and taxes may not be mentioned. Ask some questions before turning over your credit card number.

- *Is there air conditioning or a fan?* In a thatched-roof hut, air conditioning is useless because the cold air goes out through the roof.

- *Is there hot water? How is it heated?* Water heated on the roof by the sun is far cooler than water heated in a gas water tank.

- *What does "all-inclusive" mean?* Is it rice and beans for three meals a day and a lawn chair around the pool, or does it include excursions around the area?

- *Do the prices include taxes and service charges?* Tax is an additional 25%; it makes a huge difference on your bill.

- *Does the hotel accept credit cards and do they add a fee for this?* Charging for this service is against their contract with the credit card companies, but some places add this anyway.

- *How close to other places is the hotel? Will you be able to move around easily without having to pay for taxis?*

If you do book ahead, print out all correspondence and bring the documentation with you. Some proprietors have been known to offer one rate, but charge another after the customer has arrived. Make certain you read all the fine print.

If possible, book and pay for only a few days. That way, if you don't like the place, you can look around after your arrival and find another place.

See page 71 for a guideline to hotel prices.

GETTING HERE

There are many options. For a luxurious stay near the beach, you can have a tour agent from your own town book your flight and hotels so all you need to do is pack, grab your cash and credit cards, and get yourself to the airport. Or you may be on a long trip and arrive by traveling overland from the US, Guatemala or Belize. You may want to do nothing but visit one beach after another or stay on the same beach for the entire vacation. If you have specialized activities you would like to pursue, like kayaking or horseback riding, consider working with one

© 2006 HUNTER PUBLISHING, INC

of the companies that focuses on these activities. You may want to fly with a charter and return on a non-changeable date. These tickets are usually the best deal, especially if you can negotiate the flight without hotels. Be certain to confirm your return schedule at least 72 hours before departure.

BY AIR

The following airlines are the most common ones dropping into the west coast of Mexico. For more information about them, go to their websites or call them direct.

- **Aero California**, ☎ *800-237-6225 (Mx), www.aerocalifornia.de*, flies from Los Angeles and Tucson to Manzanillo, Mazatlan, Guadalajara, Puerto Vallarta, Colima and Tepic.

- **AeroMexico**, ☎ *800-237-6639 (US), 800-021-4010 (Mx), www.aeromxico.com,* flies from Los Angeles, New York, Tucson, San Diego, Dallas-Ft. Worth, Atlanta and Miami in the States and Ontario in Canada. They have flights to Guadalajara, Mazatlan and Mexico City.

- **Alaska Airlines**, ☎ *800-252-7522 (US), 800-468-2248 (US for packages), 55-5282-2484 (Mx), www.alaskaair.com*, serves 80 cities in the United States, Canada and Mexico, and has flights from Europe and Asia. I flew with them and found their prices the best, their planes full and their service exceptional, especially at the airport in Puerto Vallarta. I recommend this company.

- **American Airlines**, ☎ *800-433-7300 (US), 800-904-6000 (Mx), www.aa.com*, was one of the first airlines to fly passengers and cargo into Mexico. They fly from Dallas-Ft. Worth, Miami and Los Angeles to Mexico City, Guadalajara, Puerto Vallarta and Acapulco. In my experience, Dallas-Ft. Worth airport is

the easiest airport to get through in the
United States. The security check is efficient,
the greeters know where to send everyone,
and the people manning the stations
throughout the airport are friendly.

■ **America West**, ☎ *800-363-2597 (US), 800-
235-9292 (Mx), www.americawest.com,*
leaves from Phoenix and Las Vegas and flies
to Acapulco, Ixtapa-Zihuatenejo, Puerto
Vallarta and, through an affiliate, to
Guaymas and Guadalajara.

■ **Aviacsa**, ☎ *800-735-5396 (US), 800-711-
6733 (Mx), www.aviacsa.com.mx,* flies between Houston or Las Vegas and Mexico
City. They also offer many flights inside Mexico.

■ **British Airways**, ☎ *800-AIRWAYS (US), 55-
5387-0300 (Mx), www.ba.com,* offers three
flights a week between London and Mexico
City.

■ **Continental Airlines**, ☎ *800-231-0856 (US),
800-900-5000 (Mx), www.continental.com,*
flies from Houston and Newark to 21 destinations in Mexico, including Manzanillo and
Colima.

■ **Delta**, ☎ *800-241-4141 (US), 800-123-4710
(Mx), www.delta.com,* flies from many US areas, including Los Angeles, Dallas-Ft. Worth
and Atlanta, to Mexico City, Acapulco,
Puerto Vallarta and Guadalajara.

■ **Frontier**, ☎ *800-432-1359, www.frontierair
lines.com,* flies from select US cities to
Mazatlan, Puerto Vallarta and Ixtapa/
Zihuatenejo.

■ **Mexicana**, ☎ *800-531-7921 (US), 800-509-
8960 (Mx), www.mexicana.com,* leaves from
Los Angeles, San José, San Francisco, Oak-
land, Chicago, San Antonio, Newark, Miami,
Denver, Montreal and Toronto. There are nu-

merous cities in Central and South America from which it operates. It flies to Mexico City, Puerto Vallarta, Guadalajara and Mazatlan. Mexicana has been in business since the 1930s and has a good safety record.

▨ **United Airlines**, ☎ *800-538-2929 (US), 800-003-0777 (Mx), www.united.com,* flies from San Francisco, Chicago, Los Angeles, Washington, DC and Miami to Mexico City.

ARRIVING AT THE AIRPORT

When you fly into any Mexican airport, the procedure is simple. First, you go through Immigration, where you will receive a 90-day (usually) visitor's permit. You then pick up your bags and head for Customs inspection. You will be asked to push a button. If the light above the button turns green, you and your party are free to walk through. If it turns red, the inspectors will check your bags for any forbidden substances.

There are banks at the airports, along with some souvenir shops and places to eat, though the food is usually terrible.

To get to town, if you haven't arranged for a pick-up by one of the bigger hotels, you can take a taxi to the center. Fares are lower if you hop a cab from the street; taxis with ticket wickets at the airport are up to four times as expensive. When taking a taxi from the street, be certain to establish the price beforehand.

Taxis in Mexico are often brightly colored VW Beetles.

A bus is an option if you don't have too much luggage. Ask at the information booth in the airport which bus will take you where you want to go. Usually, the bus stops are just outside the airport, beyond the taxis on the street.

▨ OVERLAND BY BUS

Buses from other countries do not cross the border into Mexico. They leave you at the border and you must either walk across or take a local bus or taxi to the nearest bus terminal and catch a Mexican bus.

Bus travel in Mexico can be first class, second class or peasant class. The first-class buses are roomy, air-conditioned vehicles that often come with an attendant to look after your needs. The 44 reclining seats on each bus are soft. Your lunch and a drink may be included in the price of the ticket and handed to you as you board the bus. There are toilets available and, often, you can even make yourself a tea or coffee. Videos are played, usually not too loud, and they are often fairly decent and in English. Some of the companies have private waiting rooms at the bus stations, where only their passengers may sit. These companies also offer bathrooms not used by the general public in the main terminal. Second-class bus service is almost as luxurious as first class, except you don't get lunch and the bus stops at some towns on the way to your destination. They are more like the buses found in North America. Peasant-class bus travel in Mexico is most interesting, although the least comfortable. You never get a lunch or an attendant and the buses stop at many towns. No matter what class service you use, no longer do buses go only when full and carry everything, including the chicken going to market.

Ticket prices run about $5 per hour of travel for the best class and drop to just over half that for second class (usually) and even less for peasant class. It is only the peasant-class tickets that do not have reserved seats. Bus drivers are the bosses of the road and of the bus. They know their job and do it well.

Bus stations are generally large buildings on the outskirts of bigger cities. You must pay a 25¢ tax if using buses from the terminals and occasionally your carry-on luggage will be searched by security. The following companies service travel from the US border down into central Mexico.

The Estrella Blanca (Elite), ☎ *221-0850, 290-1001 or 290-1014.* Buses leave for Guadalajara, Mexico City and all major stops in-between.

Primera Plus, ☎ *221-0095, www.flecha-amarilla.com.* The ticket price includes a sandwich and juice. The air-conditioned bus is a luxury liner and comes recommended for any trips in the area if their schedule is right for you. I traveled with them and was quite pleased.

ETN, ☎ *223-5665 or 223-5666, www.etn.com.mx*, has buses going to most major destinations. This, too, is a luxury liner, but I found them less-than caring about their passengers.

Transportes del Pacifico, ☎ *222-1015 or 222-5622*, has buses going around the country often, usually once every hour to major destinations.

TAP, ☎ *290-0119*, has buses going to 24 destinations around the country. I found the workers at the PV office helpful and honest. I would not hesitate traveling with them. TAP also covers many destinations to the north like Tijuana and Guaymas.

OVERLAND BY CAR OR RV

Before entering Mexico with a vehicle you must have an American, Canadian or international driver's license. At the border you must apply for a temporary **vehicle importation permit**. For this you need proof of ownership, registra-

Border crossing.

tion, proof of citizenship and an affidavit from lien holders allowing this temporary importation. (If you take a rental car from the US or Belize into Mexico, the rental company will provide all necessary documents.) This permit is good for six months and can be used for multiple entries. The fee ($15) must be paid by Visa, MasterCard or American Express. The permit must be pasted onto the windshield. It proves that you paid to bring the vehicle in and shows the date when you must have the vehicle out of the country. If you overstay, your vehicle will be confiscated. RVs require an additional permit. It is illegal to leave your vehicle in Mexico unless you pay a 30% tax levied on the value of the vehicle.

The main roads between the American and Guatemalan border are all paved, double-lane highways. Secondary roads that follow the coast are also paved, but narrow and winding, with almost no shoulders. The speed limits, measured in kilometers, are reasonable (40-60 mph/65-100 kmh) and there are Green Angels around should you run into any mechanical problems (see page 76). Maps are accurate and signs well posted. RV parks are dotted along the coast; most allow tenting. Hotels often offer some sort of off-street parking, which is necessary if leaving the vehicle overnight.

If you have decided to bring your car, be certain it is in top shape, with good tires, a tuned-up motor, a recent carburetor overhaul, and so on. Paying for repairs at gringo prices would make this an expensive vacation. If taking a motor home, don't overload it. You can purchase anything you may want or need in Mexico and often the price will be less than at home.

INSURANCE

Mexican car insurance is essential. Foreign insurance is of no value. Offices of insurance companies line the borders for your convenience. There are two components to consider if you are involved in an accident. First, damage to the car, the property, the person, medical expenses and loss of wages. Then the moral damages are calculated. This is the pain and suffering incurred by the injured and, in Mexico, this is usually about one-third of what the actual damages are. You then have the choice of a civil or criminal case. In a criminal case, the victim receives an appointed lawyer and the liability is not limited like it is in civil cases. In the worst-case scenario, should you kill a person in an accident that you caused, you would have to pay for the damaged vehicle, the medical expenses incurred, funeral expenses and loss of wages. This would be calculated at the minimum daily wage of the person killed for a period determined by the courts. Moral damages would be added to all this. For an average person, $100,000 liability coverage should be adequate.

In the event of an accident, first and always, contact your insurance company. They know what to say and do. Do not sign anything or answer questions until you have a legal representative with you. This is your right as a driver in Mexico. If you are arrested, you have the right to be released on bail; the amount of bail is determined by a court official, not by the police. Should you be under the influence of drugs or alcohol, you may be detained for a long time.

Most of the car insurance information I used came from DriveMex.com (see below).

INSURANCE COMPANIES

There are numerous companies selling car insurance in Mexico. I recommend the following because they have built a good reputation. If you fall in with a fly-by-night company, you could lose some cash. Take the recommendations given here or those of a trusted friend.

International Insurance-Seguros, *1047 W. Madero, Mesa, AZ,* ☎ *480-345-0191, www.globalmedicalplans. com*, sells car, boat and medical insurance. They are responsive and knowledgeable. The company's owner, Patricia Romero Hamrick, is a Mexican lady with a lot of experience with insurance in Mexico. Patricia has many Mexican clients. Whenever I dealt with her, I was always satisfied. It is important to know that Mexican insurance claims can end up in court for years, whereas American claims are usually settled quickly. With this company, you can purchase insurance (dealing in English) before you head to Mexico and, since this is a Mexican company, the insurance is acceptable over the border. Their medical insurance includes emergency evacuation and reunion. That means a loved-one can join you should you be in hospital for a long time.

Sanborn's Insurance, ☎ *800-222-0158, www. sanbornsinsurance.com,* is a large company stationed in Mexico. It has been around for a long time.

Seguros Tepeyac, ☎ *800-837-3922,* was founded in 1944. It belongs to the MAPFRE system from Spain and operates in 26 countries.

DriveMex.com, ☎ *866-367-5053, www.drivemex.com,* is operated by Comerco Courtage Inc. I have worked with this company and I was pleased.

BY SEA

You can come to Mexico by private boat, public ferry or cruise ship. If taking a cruise, your agent will look after all necessary documents. All you will need is this guide-book, clothing, some money and your passport. If going by ferry between La Paz, Baja California and Mazatlan, you may find that some boats offer poor service. The business has been privatized.

The **Sematur Transbordadores Ferry** transports people and vehicles between La Paz, Baja California and Mazatlan, on the mainland, twice a week. The boat leaves at 3 pm from La Paz and the journey takes 19 hours. This was once the government-owned Caminos y Puentes Federales de Ingresos y Conexos, but the line was sold in 1989 and, since then, services have dropped. This company also runs a ferry from Santa Rosalia to Guaymas on Sunday, Tuesday and Friday, leaving from Santa Rosalia at 10 pm and returning Monday, Thursday and Saturday at 10 pm. This is a tourist-class run that takes between seven and eight hours. The cost is about $40 for adult, $20 for children, $200 for a pick-up truck and $135 for a motorcycle. The company has numerous telephone numbers in each city they service. Visit the website, www.simplonpc.co.uk/SEMATUR.html.

PRIVATE BOAT

If you are sailing your own vessel into Mexico, you will need to stop first at the Immigration office at the port of entry to get a **tourist visa** and a **temporary import permit** for your boat. You will need ownership papers proving the boat is yours or the lease agreement if the vessel is rented. You will need proof of citizenship so you can obtain a tourist visa and an arrival and departure clearance document. You must post a bond (for the value of the vessel, plus an added $10 processing fee) using a major credit card at the Banjercito bank.

You must then register your boat at a marina. If you plan to sail from one port to another, you must obtain a document specifying your arrival and departure clearances. For more specific information on sailing in Mexico, go to www.mexonline.com/boatmex.htm.

BOAT CHARTERS

Orca Sailing, *1017 15th St., Bellingham, WA,* ☎ *800-664-6049, www.orcasailing.com,* has a number of different yachts that can be rented by the week. They run between $14,000 per week for six people up to $175,000 for 12 people in a luxurious liner. The per-person cost is lower if you join a group, rather than hire the boat privately. With this company, once two people have confirmed their trip, the deal is a go. The prices include everything after you arrive at the boat's dock, even the wine with your gourmet dinners. You will be expected to help with the sailing by taking your share of the

Slow Dance *is one of Orca's vessels that sails Mexican waters.*

watch, monitoring weather, getting cyclone updates, studying the ocean currents, using SSB & VHF radios and helping with chart selection. Your route can be tailored to your specs. Equipment for high-speed watersports is included. This is a great way to see Mexico.

Cruise Ship Centers, ☎ *866-358-7285, 800-707-7327 (Canada) or 877-791-7676 (US), www.cruiseshipcenters. com,* offers three- to eight-day cruises in the Pacific, stopping at places like Puerto Vallarta, Mazatlan and Acapulco. If you wish to have your every need catered to, eat more exotic foods than your encyclopedia could list, and

still enjoy the best of Mexico, this is one option. The ships have a climbing wall, jogging tracks, mini golf, fitness and dance classes, spa facilities, pools and hot tubs, deck games, casinos, lounges, art auctions, duty-free shopping and facilities for children. The different restaurants are too many to name. The cost for one of these cruises starts at about $750 per person. I have worked with Carrol Johnson (cjohnson@cruiseshipcenters.com) for years and she has always managed to get me what I want, when I want it, for a price close to what I can afford.

Royal Caribbean, ☎ *800-511-4848*, has a three-day trip to Ensenada where you can ride horse through the hills or just sit on the beach. The ship leaves from Los Angeles. Luxurious staterooms start at $530 a day, while regular rooms cost $220 a day. This is all-inclusive. The boat has two pools, nine bars, a cinema, a fitness center, a spa, a casino and children's facilities.

GETTING AROUND

▨ BY PLANE

There are numerous companies working in Mexico. AeroMexico and Mexicana are the biggest. However,

Alaska Air, Aviacsa and Aero California also offer service to many destinations at competitive prices.

Note that ticket changes are costly in Mexico, usually running 25% of the original fare. When traveling, arrive early as your seat could be sold to someone on the standby list. Carry on as much as possible. Lost luggage is not fun. I once had all my baggage lost and it took three days to be found. During that time the airline refused to supply even a toothbrush. It was an American couple listening to my arguments with the company representative who finally produced the needed items.

See *General Directory*, page 100, for airline contact information.

▒ BY BUS

Unless you are in a hurry to get from one place to another, I suggest taking a bus. This way, you can watch the countryside, talk to locals and get to your destination feeling relaxed. Not that air travel is stressful, but bus travel is more comfortable in Mexico than it is in the US and Canada. After all, you did come to see the country.

Usually, you will find numerous bus companies going to your destination at different times during the day. If there is no direct bus, you may need to travel to the nearest city en route and connect to another bus going to your destination.

Tickets may be purchased in advance, in person. Bus companies do not take credit cards, but every bus station except in the tiniest of villages has an ATM. Baggage is labeled when you hand it over and you get a ticket that you must present to get your bags back. It is customary to give the baggage handler a few pesos for his service when putting the bags on the bus. Occasionally, you will have to go through a wand-over-body security check. Theft of baggage is not a concern.

If traveling at night, buses are comfortable, children are quiet and there are no chickens in the carry-on baggage. You may find it easier to sleep on the right-hand side of the bus, without the glare of headlights from oncoming traffic.

▨ BY CAR

For details about entering Mexico with your own car, see page 89. You can rent a vehicle from many of the main car rental companies in the US and Canada (see page 100). Privately owned companies are listed in the cities where they are located.

Mexican car insurance is essential (see page 90) and you must have a valid driver's license to rent. You must be 25 years of age or older and hold a major credit card. Remember, if you get into an accident, call the insurance company/car dealer before you answer questions or sign any papers.

> ▶▶ **AUTHOR EXPERIENCE:** *On my recent Mexico trip, I dealt with National, although I spoke with most other companies. I found that National was far more interested in telling me about the road conditions, things of which I must be aware and general information about driving in Mexico than they were in renting me a vehicle. They also gave me very good service.*

See *General Directory*, page 100, for car rental company contact information.

DRIVING

Driving is on the right, as in the US. One problem, especially if you have a large motor home, is the congestion in the towns. This congestion makes walking a hazard, never mind driving. Also, driving along the secondary roads at night should be avoided as there are always animals, one-lane bridges and cars without headlights to negotiate. There are three times as many road fatalities at night than during the day. There are also speed bumps (silent policemen) at the entrance and exit of every town and village. These should be approached slowly. Avoid parking in secluded places.

Once you arrive, if you hire a car watcher while you go into a restaurant or any other place, the watcher should get about a dollar. If you hire a valet to park your car, tip about the same.

Some basic laws you should know include:

- It is the law for drivers to fasten their seat belts, but it is not required for passengers.
- Traveling in the back of a pickup truck is legal.
- Drinking and driving is prohibited, but passengers may drink in a vehicle.
- For motorcycles, there is no helmet law.

TOLL ROADS

Be aware that most motor homes and pick-up trucks are classified as two-axle vehicles. There is always an icon beside the term describing how many axles your vehicle has and those illiterate in the language of axles can make out what they will have to pay by matching their vehicle with the icon. If you are towing a trailer or a boat, you will be charged according to the number of axles. The cost for a car

Toll road from Mexico City to Acapulco.

between Mazatlan and Culiacan is $31, and a motor home costs $35. The cost between Guadalajara and Tepic is about $35 for a car and $55 for a motor home. Go to www.mexperience.com/guide/essentials/toll_road_charges.htm and click on road charges for distances between places and the cost to travel on the toll highways. The site has other information, too. In my opinion, the amount one saves on gas, along with the savings in tranquilizers because of the better road conditions and the time saved, make the price of a toll highway well worth it.

GAS

Gasoline is available from **Pemex**, the government-owned petroleum company. Some stations have a car wash and mini-mart and offer oil changes. They sell three grades of gas. Nova is the lowest grade and price and is sold from a blue pump. RVs should not use this gas as the octane level is less than anything sold in the US or Canada and can cause knocking in the motor. Magna sin is the mid-grade fuel that is sold from the green pump. The octane level of this gas is around 86 and is probably equal to regular gas in the US or Canada. Premium gas is sold only in larger centers and is the equivalent of premium gas anywhere. Diesel is also available and is praised by drivers of RVs, who claim it is superior to American fuel in cleanliness. It is commonly recommended that RVs have a pre-filter installed and fuel/water separators to protect their pumps and injectors. Gasoline costs about 65¢ a liter/$2.75 a gallon.

POLICE/TICKETS

It was at one time common to pay the police a bribe and be on your way. This, with increased tourism, is changing. Now, if a police officer stops you and accuses you of a violation, ask for the fine. Usually, the police officer will leave you alone. If he does give you a ticket, chances are you are guilty of the crime. If you are, he will probably take your driver's license and give you a ticket. You can pay the ticket and retrieve your license at the nearest city hall. If you pay the ticket within 24 hours, it costs less than if you wait. If you are not guilty of a crime, the police officer will probably send you on your way with a warning not to do what he charged you with doing. Smile, say thank you, and be gone.

HITCHHIKING

Mexico is not a place to hitchhike. Although most Mexican families are friendly and willing to give you a ride, there is always the opportunist who will target a foreigner. Robbery or worse should always be considered. If for some reason you must hitchhike, go to a service station on the edge of town and ask for a ride from a family that is going in your direction.

AUTHOR'S TOP PICKS

1. Walk in Old Mazatlan.

2. Bird at any of the sites around **San Blas**.

3. Watch for **whales** and **turtles** along the coast.

4. Sit on the **beach** all day with a beer in hand.

Travel Information

GENERAL DIRECTORY

■ MEDICAL & HEALTH CARE

Critical Air Ambulance . . . . ☎ 800-247-8326 (US); 800-010-0268 (Mx)

Sky Med . . . . ☎ 800-475-9633 (US); 866-805-9624 (Mx)
. . . . www.skymed.com

Medic Alert. . . . . ☎ 888-633-4298 (US); www.medicalert.org

■ CAR RENTAL COMPANIES

Avis . . . . ☎ 800-288-8888 (US); 5-558-8888 (Mx); www.avis.com

Alamo . . . . ☎ 800-462-5266 (US); www.alamo.com

Budget . . . . ☎ 800-472-3325 (US); www.budget.com

Dollar . . . . ☎ 800-800-3665 (US); www.dollar.com

Hertz . . . . ☎ 800-654-3030 (US); www.hertz.com

National . . . . ☎ 800-CAR-RENT (US); www.nationalcar.com

Thrifty. . . . . ☎ 800-THRIFTY (US); www.thrifty.com

■ AIRLINES

AeroMexico . . . . ☎ 800-237-6639 (US); 800-021-4010 (Mx)
. . . . www.aeromexico.com

Alaska Airlines . . ☎ 800-252-7522 (US); 55-5282-2484 (Mx); www.alaskaair.com

America West . . . . ☎ 800-363-2597 (US); 800-235-9292 (Mx)
. . . . www.americawest.com

Aviasca . . . . ☎ 888-528-4227(US); 800-711-6733 (Mx); www.aviasca.com.mx

Continental. . . ☎ 800-231-0856 (US); 800-900-5000 (Mx); www.continental.com

Delta . . . . ☎ 800-241-4141 (US); 800-123-4710 (Mx); www.delta.com

Frontier Air . . . . ☎ 800-432-1359 (US); www.frontierairlines.com

Mexciana Airlines. . . . . ☎ 800-531-7921 (US); 800-509-8960 (Mx)
. . . . www.mexicana.com

■ EMERGENCIES WHILE IN MEXICO

Tourist Assistance . . . . ☎ 800-9-0392

Emergency Assistance (any kind) . . . . ☎ 060

■ CONSULATES

For foreign consulates, see *Consulates*, page 198, in the *Appendix*.

■ INSURANCE COMPANIES

International Insurance-Seguros . . . . ☎ 480-345-0191 (US)
. . . . www.seguros-insurance.net

Global Travel Insurance. . . . . ☎ 800-232-9415 (US)
. . . . www.globalmedicalplans.com

■ CREDIT CARD ASSISTANCE

NOTE: The telephone numbers listed above can change without notice at any time. It is best to check the Internet site for the latest telephone numbers.

VISA . . . . ☎ 800-847-2911 (US & Mx); www.visa.com	
MasterCard. . . . . ☎ 800-MC-ASSIST (US); 800-307-7309 (Mx) . . . . www.mastercard.com	
Diner's . . . . ☎ 800-234-2377; 5-258-3220 (Mx); www.dinersclub.com	
American Express . . . . ☎ 800-992-3404 (US); 336-393-1111 (collect) . . . . www.americanexpress.com	

■ USEFUL WEBSITES

www.mexonline.com
www.visitmexico.com
www.mexico.com
www.elbalero.gob.mx_kids.html. This is a great site for kids.
www.go2mexico.com
www.mexconnect.com

Travel Information

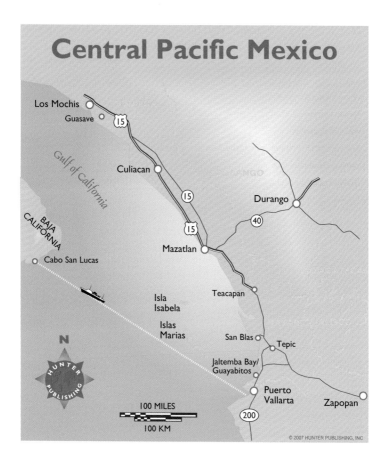

Central Pacific Mexico

Los Mochis
Guasave
15

Gulf of California

Culiacan
15

DURANGO

Durango
15
40

BAJA CALIFORNIA

15
Mazatlan

Cabo San Lucas

Isla
Isabela

Teacapan

Islas
Marias

San Blas
Tepic

N

Jaltemba Bay/
Guayabitos

HUNTER PUBLISHING

Puerto
Vallarta
Zapopan

100 MILES

200

100 KM

© 2007 HUNTER PUBLISHING, INC

Mazatlan

GETTING HERE & AROUND

▥ BY PLANE

The city is served by Aero California, Aero-Mexico, Alaska Airlines and Mexicana Airlines. The airport is 11 miles/ 18 km south of the city. A **taxi** (car) to the city center costs about $25. The more affordable taxis, called *pulmonias* (pneumonia!), cost about $5 and are actually made-over golf carts. There are also *collectivos* that leave from the front entrance to the terminal. These cost less $7.50 per person.

AIRLINE CONTACT INFORMATION	
Aero California	☎ 800-237-6225 (Mx) www.aerocalifornia.de
AeroMexico	☎ 800-237-6639 (US); 800-021-4010 (Mx) www.aeromexico.com
Alaska Airlines	☎ 800-252-7522 (US); 55-5282-2484 (Mx) www.alaskaair.com
Mexicana	☎ 800-531-7921 (US); 800-509-8960 (Mx) www.mexicana.com

■ BY BUS

The bus station is three km/two miles north of the city along Highway 15. It is a large terminal with first- and second-class areas. There is a baggage storage desk, a couple of food stalls, some souvenir shops and lots of companies vying for your business.

PULMONIAS

Pulmonias were first invented by Miguel Ramirez-urquijo in the early 1960s as a cheap method of transportation. He called them pneumonia (tongue in cheek), in Spanish. Considering the climate in Mazatlan, that is the last thing these delightful taxis would cause. They are brightly painted with things like streaks of fire, exotic birds or anything else that will make the look unique and distinct.

■ BY FERRY/BOAT

The **Baja Ferry Company**, ☎ *669-622-3390*, runs between Mazatlan and La Paz on the Baja California Peninsula, leaving Mazatlan every day at 3 pm. The terminal is at the harbor on Av Carnaval. The cost to bring a vehicle over is $250-$400, depending on size. Passengers willing to sit up all night in fairly comfortable seats pay $30; cab-

ins with private bath-
rooms are available for
about $60 per person.
The crossing takes 12
to 18 hours.

If arriving by private
boat there is an immi-
gration and customs of-
fice at the ferry slip.
Should you need to ex-
tend your visa, the staff is all too willing to help.

© Alfredo Hernandez.

BY CAR

There are numerous places to rent vehicles in Mazatlan.
The highway is not as busy as the streets in town, and
Highway 15, going both north and south from Mazatlan,
is a four-lane toll highway that is in excellent condition.

CAR RENTAL COMPANIES

They are all here: Budget, Hertz, Avis, National
and so on. If you book from one of the large hotels, you will have to use the company they work
with. I mention just a couple here to give an idea
of prices and types of cars available.

AGA Rent-a-Car, *at the airport,* ☎ *669-981-3580,
or on Av Culiacan and Mochis,* ☎ *669-914-4405,
www.agarentacar.com.mx*, has small cars for
rent. Smaller vehicles are a good option here because they are easier to maneuver around the
maniac city drivers. The approximate price for a
Volkswagen is $400 a week and a Jetta Stratus
is about $950. Insurance is extra.

Budget Car Rentals, *Av Camaron Sabalo #402,
Zona Dorada,* ☎ *669-913-2000, or at the airport,*
☎ *669-982-1220,* has cars with unlimited mile-
age, automatic transmission and air conditioning. They can be rented from the airport for
$200-$400 a week, depending on the size of the
vehicle. Insurance is extra.

Mazatlan

Rent-A-Ride, *Av Camaron Sabalo #204, Lomas Plaza (next to Kelly's Bike Shop)*, ☎ *669-913-1000*, has 150 to 1500 cc motorbikes. You can rent them for four hours or up to a week, or take a guided motorcycle tour to Copala, Concordia or La Noria. You must have a motorcycle license to qualify. I have no prices for the bikes, which all appeared to be in good condition. However, be aware that I know zip about motorbikes.

SERVICES

Police Station, *Calle Ruiz and Santa Monica, Zona Dorada,* ☎ *669-903-9200.*

The **Tourist Office** *is on the 4th floor of the Banrural Bldg, Av Sabalo and Tiburon,* ☎ *669-916-5166,* two blocks past El Cid Resort.

The **post office**, *Calle Florez and Juarez,* ☎ *669-981-2121, Monday to Friday, 8 am-5 pm, Saturday until 1 pm.* Red mailboxes are along sidewalks everywhere in town.

Head to **Hospital Sharp**, *Calle Kumate and Bueina near Zaragoza Park,* ☎ *669-986-5676 or 986-7911,* if you have an emergency. There is a lab, X-ray and intensive care services available here. English is spoken.

Polimedica, ☎ *669-913-9984, annachangmd@red2000.com.mx*, is a plastic surgeon should you want a tummy tuck, breast enlargement, face lift or any other type of reconstruction. Mazatlan is a choice place to recover from something like this.

The **Tourist Emergency Hotline**, ☎ *078*, is for tourists who run into problems. The line features bilingual operators who can provide information or transfer emergency calls to the appropriate agency. This is a 24-hour, seven-day-a-week service.

PUBLICATIONS

Pacific Pearl, *www.pacificpearl.com*, lists lots of event times and dates and also has a want-ad section.

Mazatlan Interactive has information about events, such as the annual triathlon, and columns with Mexican recipes.

Complete Guide to Mazatlan, by Oses Cole Isunza and written in English, is a little red pamphlet you'll see at tour offices and some hotels. For those wanting more history than my book can supply, Isunza's book is the one. It is not expensive ($10) and the proceeds go to the Red Cross of Mazatlan. The book is very well researched and has an infinite amount of historical details about the city. There is also a map at the back indicating where all the important buildings are located in Old Mazatlan.

SIGHTSEEING

OLD MAZATLAN

This area was in total disrepair until the 1980s when a group of wise citizens realized that the old buildings were, in fact, cultural history and needed to be salvaged. Today, the transformation has occurred and walking, sitting, eating or touring in this area is a must for at least a few days. It will seem as though you have entered a time warp and gone back a hundred years; the modern conveniences incorporated into the restorations are non-intrusive. The buildings are pastel-colored with wrought iron bars decorating the windows and plaques identifying where you are. The streets are narrow and the plazas usually have restaurants with tables on the street.

 Viejo Mazatlan is a locally produced paper that features historical stories about things like the coming of the Japanese after World War II or the first writers to the city and what they said about the place. Be certain to read this and patronize some of the events listed.

SINALOA TAMBORA

The Sinaloa tambora is the type of band you'll hear playing around Mazatlan. It was first started in the early 1900s when a group of Germans came from Bavaria to open a brewery. They couldn't live without their "oompah-pah," so the music was quickly adopted and incorporated into Mexican music. Today it is a unique sound that is part German, part Mexican.

Plaza Revolucion, has *Calles Angel Florex, Guillermo Nelson, 21 de Marzo and Benito Juarez* along its four sides. This was once the site of the city's market, but now it has numerous laurel trees interspersed with park benches. These surround a kiosk built in 1909 with 4,000 pesos left by a German merchant commemorating his own 50th birthday. The kiosk was built 13 years after the municipality received the funds.

Building of the **Cathedral of the Immaculate Conception**, at one end of the square, was started in 1856 but not completed until 1899. It was delayed because the Laws of the Reform caused confusion as to the allocation of funds. It was under the pressure of Father Miguel Lacarra, who wanted the building finished, that the work was completed. The two towers weren't finished until the mid-1890s. This was because of politics between the designer and the priests of the parish. Inside, the cathedral has three naves and a gothic altar. There are statues of saints and angels carved from white Italian marble.

There are four side altars in the church and the tomb of Miguel Franco, the first Bishop of the dioceses of Mazatlan. The main altar is made from Carrera marble and crystal chandeliers light the main aisle. The pipe organ came from Paris and was first played in the church in 1889. The stone that is so prominent in the arches and columns is from a nearby quarry. The cathedral, like many parts of Old Mazatlan, is being restored to its original grandeur.

Mazatlan's impressive cathedral.

Palacio Federal, *east side of the plaza*, is a modern two-story building that was constructed in the 1940s. It has the post office inside. **City Hall**, built in the 1850s, is also on the plaza. It houses most of the elected municipal representatives. In the mayor's office is an exceptional portrait of Miguel Hidalgo, the father of Mexican Independence. The balcony overlooking the square is where the Grito ceremony takes place every September 15. The ceremony commemorates the call to arms made by Hidalgo in 1810 that finally resulted in independence.

Plaza Mochada, *Av Miguel Aleman*, is the oldest plaza in the city. Today it is lined with restaurants, most of which have seating on or near the street. There is only one road past the plaza so traffic is low, the square unpolluted and quiet. This is a very bohemian place to sit at any time of day. Nearby restaurants are Pedro and Lola, Altazor Arz, El Cielo, Nikoy Suchi and Café Pacifico.

The land holding the plaza was originally a swamp, but city officials in the early 1800s closed a saltwater channel that fed the area and let the land dry. The land was donated to the city by Juan Nepomuceno Machado, a rich merchant originally from the Philippines who made his fortunes in Mazatlan. Just off the plaza is the bust of Romana de la Peña de Careaga, the founder of the city's orphanage. Across from the bust is the Angela Peralta Theatre, an active performing and visual arts center.

Angela Peralta Theatre, *Calle Carnival #47, just off Plaza Mochada, no phone,* was the dream of Manuel Rubio who, in 1869 bought the property and started the construction. He died when the ship he was traveling on sank, so his widow had the theater finished and, in 1874, it opened. However, due to financial difficulty, she couldn't keep it running, so she sold it to Martin Mendia, who did some work to the building and again sold it, probably at a handsome profit, to Juan Bautista. Under that directorship the theater flourished and became the best performing arts center in western Mexico. In 1943, its name was changed to honor the singer who never managed to sing on its stage. Angela Peralta and her entourage of 76 people came to the city to perform but died during Mazatlan's yellow fever epidemic.

THE MEXICAN NIGHTINGALE

Soprano Angela Peralta was dubbed the Mexican Nightingale when she mesmerized European audiences with her voice. She was just 16 years of age. In 1873 she did a second tour of Europe and sang with Aida with Verdi as conductor. She not only sang, but she also composed operas. After a famous life peppered with scandals, Peralta died in Mazatlan in1883 at the age of 38.

During a hurricane in 1975, the building was destroyed and lay in ruin until the mid-1980s, when all of Old Mazatlan was under restoration. It took from 1987 to 1992 for the building to be reconstructed.

Before entering the theater, visit the exhibition gallery to view temporary exhibits and old photos showing the building's history. There is also an extensive display of

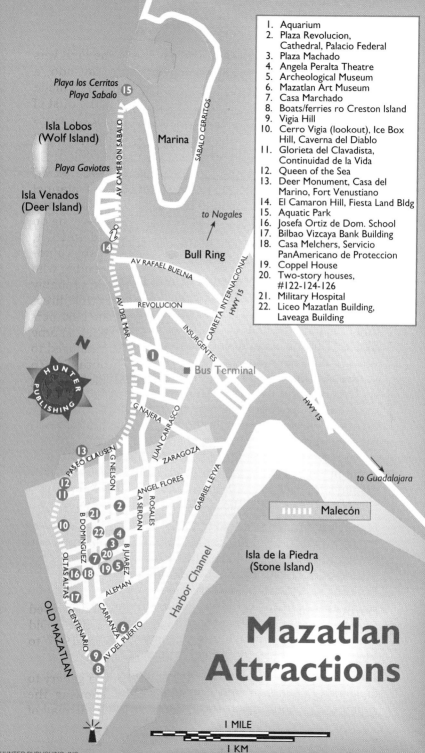

1. Aquarium
2. Plaza Revolucion, Cathedral, Palacio Federal
3. Plaza Machado
4. Angela Peralta Theatre
5. Archeological Museum
6. Mazatlan Art Museum
7. Casa Marchado
8. Boats/ferries ro Creston Island
9. Vigia Hill
10. Cerro Vigia (lookout), Ice Box Hill, Caverna del Diablo
11. Glorieta del Clavadista, Continuidad de la Vida
12. Queen of the Sea
13. Deer Monument, Casa del Marino, Fort Venustiano
14. El Camaron Hill, Fiesta Land Bldg
15. Aquatic Park
16. Josefa Ortiz de Dom. School
17. Bilbao Vizcaya Bank Building
18. Casa Melchers, Servicio PanAmericano de Proteccion
19. Coppel House
20. Two-story houses, #122-124-126
21. Military Hospital
22. Liceo Mazatlan Building, Laveaga Building

Playa los Cerritos
Playa Sabalo

Isla Lobos
(Wolf Island)

Playa Gaviotas

Isla Venados
(Deer Island)

Marina

to Nogales

Bull Ring

AV CAMERON SABALO
SABALO CERRITOS
AV RAFAEL BUELNA
REVOLUCION
AV DEL MAR
INSURGENTES
CARRETA INTERNACIONAL HWY 15

HUNTER PUBLISHING

N

Bus Terminal

HWY 15

to Guadalajara

⣿⣿⣿ Malecón

G NAJERA
JUAN CARRASCO
ZARAGOZA
PASEO CLAUSEN
G NELSON
ANGEL FLORES
ROSALES
A SERDAN
GABRIEL LEYVA
B DOMINGUEZ
OLTAS ALTAS
CENTENARIO
B JUAREZ
ALEMAN
CARRANZA
AV DEL PUERTO

Isla de la Piedra
(Stone Island)

Harbor Channel

OLD MAZATLAN

Mazatlan Attractions

1 MILE

1 KM

carnival costumes. There is a $2 charge to tour the theater if you are not attending a concert.

The theater seats 840 people and you can get cubicles where your party can sit separate from the rest of the audience, much like they did 200 years ago in theaters across Europe. These cubicles are complete with red velvet curtains held in place with gold ropes and tassels. Elegant! The theater is open about an hour before public performances. Check the posters outside or with the tourist office for performance times.

The **Church of San José**, *Calle Neveria and La Campaña.* Constructed in 1835, this is the oldest church in town. Although tiny, it is one of the nicer churches in the area.

The **Archeological Museum of Mazatlan**, *Sixto Osuna #72, ☎ 669-985-3502, 10 am-6 pm daily, except Mondays, Sunday until 3 pm, $5.* The museum is in a restored building constructed in 1904 as the home of Marcos Elorza. There is a small collection of Indian artifacts and some collected items of the city's chronicler, Miguel Valdes. Of the three salons, the first holds mostly ceramics from around the state. The second has clothes made from cotton and animal skins, lace collars and ornaments used to decorate the body. The third has mostly funereal objects, including urns and objects needed while traveling in the afterlife, such as jewelry and personal belongings that were precious to the deceased. The displays are well organized and there is a bookstore with English publications about Mexican art and history.

Mazatlan Museum of Art, *Calle Venustiano Carranza #1, no phone, open daily except Monday, 10 am-6 pm, and Sunday until 3 pm,* is located in a historic building constructed in 1896 by an old ship-owning family. The building was taken over by the government, restored and made the cultural center in 1998. Today you can see paintings from well-known artists such as José Luis Cuevas, Rufino Tamayo and Francisco Goitia. There is also a room dedicated to local artists.

Casa Machado, *Calles Heriberto Frias, Sixto Osuna, Belisario Dominguez and Constitución, no phone, 9 am-6 pm daily,* contains furniture and artifacts from Old

Mazatlan. This huge building, also called Portales de Canobbio, is named after the family who owned it for about 150 years. It was Benito Machado and his brother Juan Nepomuceno (I too don't see the connection in family names) who ran a trading house in the building. It changed hands occasionally until 1830, when Tomasa Ostuna got hold of it and became the only legal seller of footwear in the city. The *casa* was expanded and thus started the world-famous shoe store business. Eventually, the house was willed to the wife of Luis Canobbio (aha – the connection) and they opened a pharmacy in part of the building. This family also developed some medical remedies that earned them a fortune.

There's a **bullfighting** ring at Av Rafael Buelna at the Plaza Monumental. Bullfights are held every Sunday starting at 4 pm sharp from Christmas to Easter. This is an old Latin spectator sport that is distasteful to some but should be viewed with an open mind at least once. The bull, once killed, is used to feed the less fortunate. The cost for this event is $25 per person and usually three bulls are killed each week.

TERMS OF BULLFIGHTING

- **Banderilleros** are the men who assist the matador in positioning the bull in the ring.
- **Banderillas** are the short swords used by the *banderilleros* to stab the bull.
- A **corrida** is a bullfight.
- The **matador** is an experienced bullfighter who is always dressed in an elaborate outfit.
- The **picador** is the fighter who, from the back of a horse, stabs the bull in the neck and shoulder muscles.
- **Sorteo** is the process of choosing a bull for a *matador*.
- **El toro** is the bull.

Mazatlan

A fight has three stages. The first is when the bull is rushed into the arena to display his powers and two *picadors* thrust lances into its shoulders. The second stage is when the *banderilleros* stick long darts into the shoulders to debilitate the animal. The final stage is announced by trumpets. This is when the *matador* dodges and taunts the dying bull.

ADVENTURES ON FOOT

■ ALONG THE MALECÓN

The *malecón* is one of the nicest in Mexico, starting in the old city and working 12 miles/20 km up the coast to the big hotels. There are historical viewpoints, statues and palapa-hut restaurants along the way. Some of the beaches are great for cooling off, while others are best for surfing. It is a good day's easy exercise to walk from one end to the other and then take a bus/taxi back.

I will start my description of the town at the south end of the *malecón* in Old Mazatlan where the ferry crosses over to **Creston Island**. The island has **El Faro**, set on a hill just over 500 feet/150 meters high. Many consider this the tallest working lighthouse in the world. Light projected from the lighthouse can reach 36 miles/45 km out to sea. There are restaurants at the jetty, along with numerous boats ready to take you to the islands just offshore.

Following **Centenario Blvd**, named so because it was finished during the 100-year anniversary of Mexico's independence, climb Vigia Hill on the opposite side of the road to the ocean. On the hill is an old British canon manufactured in the 1800s. This lookout is where the colonists kept vigil for pirates coming into the bay, and used the cannon on them. Looking from the top of the hill, the two white islands covered in guano, called the Two Sisters, are impressive. The third island, from November to May, holds a colony of sea lions.

Where the *malecón* turns into **Olas Altas Blvd** and joins Olas Altas Bay (means "big waves") is the Shield of the

The malecón *has many art pieces along its route.*

State. The bay here is good for surfers and you will often see surfing classes taking place in the waters protected by rocks that form the barrier between the two bays.

The oval **shield** has the Mexican eagle on top with a snake in his mouth. Under the snake, in the oval area, is the name of the state and on the bottom is the date that state entered the federation. The oval is divided into four equal sections and represents the cities of Mazatlan with the deer, El Fuerte with the fort, Culiacan with the anchor and Rosario with the sheep. The shield is made of ceramic tiles.

Olas Altas in 1862 was victory square when the Mexicans expelled the French. The celebrations lasted 15 days, during which time tents were put along the street to hold restaurants, saloons and ice cream parlors. There were street musicians, fireworks and betting games. Tourism in the 1960s caused the transformation of the area, and now the street is full of hotels, restaurants, marinas and commercial housing developments.

Continuing along the avenue, but before Calle Angel Florez, are two old mansions. One, built in 1904 by Marcos Elorza, is now the archeological museum (see page 112), and the second is the Angela Peralta theater started in 1869 and completed in 1874 (see page 110).

After the next small point in the bay is **Ice Box Hill**, on the opposite side of the road to the ocean. This is where city residents once kept ice imported from San Fran-

Hiker at Devil's Cave.

cisco. The coolness of the inner mountain kept the ice solid for a long time. At the base of the hill is a barred-off entrance called the **Caverna del Diablo** (Devil's Cave), where colonists kept ammunition in the days when the cannon on Vigia Hill was in full use.

Across from the hill is the bronze monument to the **Women of Mazatlan**. They appear to be sea nymphs, and look very sexy with their outstretched arms and clinging robes.

Just beyond the monument is the **Glorieta del Clavadista**, the cliff where divers plunge into the swirling waters below. The trick is to dive just when the waves are at their highest below the cliffs. If they miscalculate, the water won't be deep enough and they will crash onto the rocks. At one time this was a trade where divers went into the water for coins thrown by spectators, but now they do it for entertainment and collect the coins personally. To watch them is breathtaking. They perform twice daily, once at 11 am and once at 1 pm. Next to the cliff is the **Continuidad de la Vida** (Continuation of Life) statue with plunging and diving dolphins representing life. Up from the dolphins is the **Queen of the Sea**, a little mermaid with cupid beside her.

The *malecón* turns east at this point and the name changes to **Claussen Blvd**. Just before it turns is the monument to the deer.

Dolphin fountain and statue along the malecón.

▶▶ **LOCAL LINGO:** Mazatlan *means "Place of the Deer" in local Nahuatl language.*

On the point across from the deer are two mansions standing alone. One is the **Casa del Marino**, House of the Sailors, where visiting sailors could stay as guests of the city. The second one is **Fort Venustiano Carranza**, built after the French left. There is a sheltered cove along the beach called Playa Los Piños, another surfing beach. The second cliff forming this cove is Punta Tiburon, where the University of Sinaloa has its marine sciences building. You will often see students on the rocky shore working on projects.

The next stretch follows Av del Mar. This is the longest bay in Mazatlan; it starts at Tiburon and goes all the way to **El Camaron Hill**, five miles/eight km away. Long ago this bay was called San Felix Bay and the port at one end was called Puerto Viejo, but now the beach is simply called North Beach.

This stretch of beach is where the more expensive hotels and trendy restaurants are located. It is also where joggers, entertainers and fishermen congregate once the sun falls below the waters.

Near the far end of the *malecón* is Punta del Camaron with the **Fiesta Land** building, a Moorish-styled complex with hotel, restaurants, discos and bars. It is a landmark that is easily seen from most parts of the city. You have now entered the Golden Zone, where **Playa Las Gaviotas** and **Playa Sabalo** offer their clean beaches and soft surf for swimming. North of Camino Real is **Playa Los Cerritos** (Little Hills Beach), where the sand and sea stretch for six miles/10 km. This is one of my favorite areas because it is isolated and exceptionally clean.

HISTORICAL HOUSE TOUR

This may be the only city in the country that boasts a walking tour of historical houses, all researched and recorded by Oses Cole Isunza in his book (see page 193). There are almost 40 buildings mentioned in the book; I describe only a few here. Unless there is a sign and ticket box outside the house, it is not open to visitors. Those that are open charge $2-$5 per person. Whether you enter or not, the houses are interesting to look at and to photograph. I like to speculate on what life was like over a century ago in Mexico and these buildings give me lots to think about.

Josefa Ortiz de Dominguez School, *Olas Altas at the ocean*, was built by Natividad Gonzalez at the end of the 1800s. The man's initials are still visible in the wrought iron of the upper windows. The building covers an entire city block and was regarded as decadent even in pre-Revolutionary times. It was confiscated during the revolution. You can enter the halls and look at the basic construction of the building but, since this is an operating school, you cannot enter the classrooms.

Bilbao Vizcaya Bank Building, *Olas Altas #67,* has been a bank since the 1920s. The building was originally constructed in 1870, as a private residence by John Kelly, the British Consul to Mazatlan. In 1910 Grandfather Rico, ancestor of the present owners, bought privately issued bank notes belonging to this banking company. Due to political upheaval, the value of the notes depreciated.

SMART DEAL

As the value of the bank notes dropped, Señor Rico was able to purchase enough of the money to exchange it for the deed of the property. The bank owners originally believed that Mr. Rico would pay in silver.

Telleria House, *Calles Malpica and Olas Altas,* was built in the early 1900s as a private residence. The unique aspect of this building is that it appears to have a basement, something not built in homes around Mazatlan. Two granite support beams hold the roof of the terrace.

Casa Melchers, *corner of Constitución and Venus*, was built in 1846 for the German Merchant Company. The two dwellings were for the manager and the clerks, who were brought from Europe during those days. This company flourished and by the 1900s offered the first automobiles for sale in Mexico. Locals would go out of their way to pass the building so they could gawk at the new form of transportation. John Bradbury bought the first vehicle and he transferred it on carts drawn by oxen to Rosario, where he lived. After the 1929 market crash the building became a warehouse that finally burned down.

Mazatlan

It was rebuilt as a truck assembly plant and then it was abandoned. Tunnels under the buildings were used by the merchants, during political upheavals, to transfer smuggled merchandise from one hiding spot to another in order to escape taxation from the new authorities.

Servicio Panamericano de Proteccion Bldg, *Constitución and Venus, opposite Casa Melchers,* is the two-story building built in the early 1900s. It was originally the Bank of London and Mexico. After the revolution it became the Bank of Mexico and then the Mexican version of Brinks, the Servicio Panamericano de Proteccion.

Coppel House, *Calle Constituccion #118,* was built by Luis Fontana between 1865 and 1870 as his primary residence. He sold it in 1878 to a man called Juan B. Acosta, who changed it to its present design. The design of the balcony with its massive cornices is of special interest.

Two-story Houses, *Calle Mariano Escobedo, numbers 122-124-126,* were built in 1865 for Federico Ymaña, who owned the local hat factory. The gargoyles on the ironworks are interesting.

> **FACT FILE:** *The rust on the iron at the two-story houses is an indication that the pieces are from Europe, because the ones made in Mexico are alloyed so that they don't rust.*

Military Hospital, *Calles Venus and Angel Flores,* was built in the mid-1850s and is one of the oldest hospitals in western Mexico. Part of the present structure is new, but was built in the old architectural style. Along one side of the building you can see tree roots imbedded into the wall. This is a fascinating building and, if you have a special interest in architectural design, ask permission to enter. You may be granted entrance to the vegetated courtyard.

Liceo Mazatlan Bldg., *Calle Constitución and Niños Heroes,* was a trading house constructed by prosperous merchant Elorza, Lejarza and Compañia and finished in 1900. It remained a trading house until the 1960s when the company relocated. The iron balconies and window frames along the second floor are of special interest.

Laveaga House, *Constitución and Niños Heros, across from Liceo Bldg.,* was built by José Vicente de Laveaga, a rich mining baron of the 1850s. After he built it as his residence, he made himself into a private banker and conducted his business on the lower level of the house. When the French arrived in 1862, he liquidated his assets and headed for California to live (and die).

GOLF

Estrella del Mar Golf Course, *Isla de Piedra,* ☎ *669-982-3300, www.estrelladelmar.com,* is an 18-hole, par 72 course designed by Robert Trent Jones. It sits on 175 acres of prime real estate right on the beach on Isla de Piedra (Stone Island) and is said to be better in price, service and scenery (most holes overlook the ocean) than any course in Puerto Vallarta. They offer a special twilight rate (18 holes, $69) and a "discount Wednesday" (18 holes, $82.50, 25% off regular cost). Golf lessons are available from the John Jacobs' Golf School.

The 8th hole.

Campestre Mazatlan Golf Course and Country Club, *Camino International South at Km 1195,* ☎ *669-980-1570, 7 am-6 pm daily,* is an older, nine-hole course that costs about $15 per person to play. Caddies are available.

El Cid Country Club, *7 am-5:30 pm,* was designed by Larry Hughes and Lee Trevino. This course is available only to El Cid guests. Some of the greens are slick, while others are a bit shaggy. The tee boxes are poor.

You must use a caddy provided by El Cid (and pay for him). All reports I have gotten indicate that this isn't the best course in town. However, the annual tournaments held here every March and November offer thousands of dollars in prizes as well as carts and vacation packages. There is also a driving range, putting greens and a short-game area.

■ TENNIS

Sports World Kaoz, *Av Rafael Buelna, behind the bull-ring,* is in the sport complex. Three hard courts are open to the public, plus there is a pool with water slides, a squash court, a football and soccer field, a snack bar and a lounge.

ADVENTURES ON WATER

Aquarium, *Av de Los Deportes #111,* ☎ *669-981-7816, 9:30 am-6 pm daily, entry $5 for adults and $2 for children.* The aquarium has a botanical garden at its entrance and is guarded by a few old crocodiles. The aquarium has over 250 species of fish from around the world, a marine-life presentation area where you can watch films about the ocean, and a sea lion show that is a big attraction to youngsters. The shows are three-in-one: the first starts at 10:30 am when the diver feeds the shark; at 11 am the sea lions perform; and at 11:30 parrots do their entertaining. This is repeated two more times throughout the day. There is also an art gallery. The gardens have an aviary with eagles, hawks and peacocks, as well as turtles. A tour and show takes about three hours. At the entrance to the aquarium is a statue of three kids. They are on each others' shoulders, trying to feed a dolphin that is jumping out of the water.

The aquarium is the home of the rehabilitation center called Friends of the Aquarium, www.mexonline.com/acuario.htm. This non-profit organization takes and cares for injured or mistreated parrots, birds of prey, ducks and pelicans. It was started by biologist Sandra Guido and American Kittie Jepsen, and has attracted veterinarians, educators and marine biologists to help with the work. To visit them and offer help of any kind (the best is always financial) will assist a few more birds survive.

Across the street is the statue of Don Cruz Lizarraga, founder of the famous band El Recordo. The statue has Lizarraga standing with a clarinet in his hand and a tuba and snare drum at his side.

Aquatic Park Mazagua, *at Sabalo Cerritos,* ☎ *669-988-0041, from 10 am-6 pm daily.* There are water slides, a wave pool and a shallow river for youngsters to float through with their safety devices well in place. There are diving boards and a waterfall. First built in 1989 with kids in mind, the park is a toddler-friendly place with numerous climbing areas shaped in the forms of different animals.

OFFSHORE ISLANDS

Deer Island is reached by boat from the waterfront at El Cid. The boat is a World War II amphibious landing craft called the Duck and painted to look like a shark with its mouth open. It leaves the dock at 10 am, noon and 2 pm and costs $8 round trip. The last boat back is at 4 pm. You can also rent a kayak ($10 an hour) or Hobie Cat ($30 an hour, up to four people) from numerous places along the beach and paddle or sail over to Deer Island (the distance is very short). El Cid can provide a tillerman with their Hobie Cats. The island itself has volleyball nets on

Kayakers paddle to Deer Island

the beach. Snorkeling is best to the left when facing the water. Where the rocks start getting big you will see red sea fans, sponges, conch and tropical fish. There are also some turtles, eagle rays (rare) and tons of tropical fish. As you pass the point, the water gets rougher, the rocks bigger and the fish larger. In the opposite direction, to the south, there is a rock shelf with sea urchins. In the center of the island are rock paintings of historical value. Ask directions from your boatman. Two other islands – Bird Island and Wolf Island – also have nice beaches and can be reached on the Duck.

Stone Island is accessed by water taxi ($1, round trip) that leaves from the ferry slip at the end of the bus line. Take the bus marked Sabalo Centro. On your way over, dolphins will often follow the boat. The island has nine miles/15 km with beaches, trees and open-air restaurants. When you arrive, go straight ahead for the restaurant area and go to the right for a bay that offers good

snorkeling and gentle waves. On a mild day, going to the deeper water where the rocks are bigger and the swells stronger is advisable. There is a coconut plantation on the island (turn left from the boat landing) where you can rent horses for an hour or two.

Stone Island ferry terminal.

▸▸ **AUTHOR NOTE:** *All the restaurants near the boat landing serve delicious food. Please do not bring your own lunch, as the economy of the island is delicate and your contribution by way of buying a meal is greatly appreciated. You will find the prices less than those along the* malecón *in town.*

Tourists from the hotels and cruise ships arrive on Stone Island in the morning and usually leave by 5 pm.

Also on the island is the **Estrella del Mar Golf Course**, *Isla de la Piedra,* ☎ *669-982-3300, www.estrelladelmar. com,* an 18-hole, par 72 green designed by Robert Trent Jones. See page 121. The same beach resort has 26 suites and 22 villas, all with air conditioning, dishwashers, BBQ grills, stereos, king-sized beds, toasters, ceiling fans, cable TV, cooking utensils and coffee makers. High-season rates run $115-$249 per person, per day, with a substantial discount for bookings of a week or more. There is a minimum stay of three nights. Also see *Places to Stay*, below, for details about the Hilton Estrella del Mar.

El Patio Restaurant, along the strip near the boat landing, has both international and Mexican dishes for reasonable prices.

■ BEACHES

Playa Olas Altas in the Old Town is good for surfers because the waves are consistently high. Boogie boarding and body surfing for experienced swimmers is good here. It is not a recommended area for swimming or snorkeling.

Playa Los Piños is also a surfing beach. It is rocky, so it has some eddies where you can get calmer water; the surfing section starts at the cliff where the water is calm. You will often see surfing classes in this area. Some anglers cast from the rocks on the north side of this beach.

Rocky shore.

BEACH DANGER FLAG SYSTEM

There is a system of red, yellow and white flags that indicates possible dangers in the water.

■ RED – The undercurrent is dangerous to swimmers and under no circumstances should you go into the area between the two red flags. Undertow is not to be ignored; it has caused many deaths.

■ YELLOW – Jellyfish are in the area. To avoid being stung, do not go into the water between the two yellow flags.

■ WHITE – The white flags mean there is some soft surf, but have fun.

Playa Norte is the long (five miles/7.5 km) stretch along the *malecón*. Once past the fishing-boat area at the south end, the sand is kept fairly clean. There are many palapa-hut restaurants along this beach. The swells in the water are gentle and good for swimming. The waves at the north end of this beach are good for beginner surfers.

Playa Camaron in Zona Dorado starts around Valentinos, also where the luxurious hotels start. The water at Camaron is rough and not for swimmers or surf-ers with average skill. The beach is narrow and consists mainly of crushed shells.

Playa Las Gaviotas starts where the beach levels off and becomes much wider, and the water becomes gentle. This stretch is exceptionally calm because it is protected by offshore islands. This beach is good for swimming, but the waves are not strong enough for surfing.

Playa Sabalo goes past the Camino Real to the tidal la-goon on the north end. The beach lagoon is good and the lagoon itself is a popular birding spot. The waters be-tween here and Los Cerritos are often dotted with windsurfers.

Playa Los Cerritos is beyond Camino Real. Here, the tourists thin out. Although there are a few palapa huts, it is mainly undeveloped and good for beachcombing. This is a long walk from the center of town.

SPORTFISHING

Fishing is popular around the bay. The big catches are marlin, sailfish, dorado and tuna. Catch and release only. You might also find mahi-mahi, sea bass, wahoo and rooster fish.

ADVENTURES IN NATURE

Teacapán can be visited as a day trip from Mazatlan. It is an expanse of palm groves, mangroves, estuaries and lagoons, called the lungs of Mexico. About 95 miles/140 km of wetland can be traveled by boat. People do so in search of birds mainly,  but also lizards, iguanas, snakes and insects. For the botanist, the interesting vegetation is limitless. You can also rent bikes, horses and kayaks, or take a boat to Isabel Island to see sea lions and whales during their migratory season. You can also visit Bird Island and, en route, pass by Sea Shell Hill, an odd piece of land made entirely of crushed shells.

Playa/**Laguna Caimanero** area is now under environmental control because of the vast numbers of migratory birds that pass through. During wet years, the numbers increase from hundreds to thousands. The town of Caimanero is at the south end of a huge sand dune that separates Laguna Caimanero from the beach. The lake is about 50 miles/75 km long and five miles/eight km wide, but only three inches/eight cm deep. This lake in the past was used for hunting, but that sport has been abolished.

Mazatlan

▶▶ **BIRD WATCH:** *The thorn bush beyond Caimanero Lake is known to hold the rare chuck-aucka. This bird closes its eyes while it sings, making it easy to hunt.*

There are small palapa-hut restaurants at the south end of the lake where you can eat, but there is no place to stay unless you have your own tent. Water must be carried in, as there are no freshwater streams along the beach.

ADVENTURES OF THE BRAIN

Centro de Idiomas de Mazatlan, *Belisario Dominguez #190,* ☎ *669-985-5606, www.spanishlink.org,* offers courses designed for serious participants who need a working knowledge of conversational Spanish in a short period of time. There are a maximum of six students per class, and the main focus is on speaking and listening. Opened in 1973, this school has won the International Committee of Quality Award twice, plus the Quality and Prestige Award from the Mexican National Chamber of Commerce. Courses start every Monday and you should enroll by the Saturday before. There is no compensation if your classes fall during national holidays. The cost is $30 to register, plus $150 per week for four hours of intensive study per day. Private lessons cost $330 a week for four hours a day. Books are $20 extra. Should you study longer than a week, a discount is offered.

Mazatlan Reading Library, *Sixto Osuna #115, corner of Carranza, next to the Archeological Museum, MazLibrary@ mexconnect.com,* is run by an energetic and knowledgeable man by the name of Joe Ketchum. If there is anything you want to know that I have not included in this book, ask Joe – he'll know the answer. You can borrow from the fairly extensive non-profit library designed to gather and maintain a collection of writing in English or Spanish. The library cooperates with schools to promote reading and will provide information to anyone. It has over 4,000 titles, most in English, mostly fiction. You can become a member for $25 a year, which would include two adults and minor children of the same household. Additional adults in the same family pay just $5 extra per year. Short-term visitors pay $5 per month. The library is run by volunteers and they encourage you to borrow books, offer a few hours of work or just donate money and books. It's a great place to sit around and talk.

DAY TRIPS

Below, I have listed villages that can be visited as a day trip from Mazatlan. However, you can also go to many of them and stay for more than a day. This is recommended so that you get a better idea of what Mexico is really about. Plus, you get to spread the buck a bit, so more people benefit from your visit.

EL QUELITE

El Quelite is 20 miles/33 km north of Mazatlan across the Tropic of Cancer and on El Quelite River. This tiny colonial town can easily be reached by local bus or car. There is a nice walk, up the hill that has the stations of the cross, for views of the area. The **church** on the plaza has some paintings from the 1600s. This is an excellent place to get the flavor of "Old Mexico," have a bite to eat, and take some good photos. If you want to stay the night, there are two small hotels in town – **Meson de los Laureanos** and **Meson de Doña Mercedes**. You will have to look at both and see which one you prefer.

ESTACION DIMAS

Estacion Dimas is just 45 miles/60 km north of Mazatlan, where there are the **Piedra Labradas**, ancient stone carvings lying on the beach. These huge, black volcanic rocks have numerous designs and are considered some of the best examples of rock art in Mexico. Some believe that the carvings are from the Toltec civilization. Near the stone carvings is **Barra Piaxtla**, natural stone arches in the sea. Because of the proximity of the two, it is thought this may be a holy place. Archeologists believe these stones were carved about 1500 BC. Occasionally, they are covered by a high tide; this is, evidently, one of the reasons they are in such good shape.

PETROGLYPHS 101

The earliest petroglyphs were carved about 40,000 years ago in Australia. Eventually, about 17,000 years ago, the work evolved and teachers used carved slates so they could carry their works with them. This development happened throughout the world, including Mexico.

There are five subjects that are used in 80% of all rock art. They are warriors (as single soldiers or armies), animals (either real or mythical), wood-and-stone houses, symbolic inscriptions and weapons. Some of the stones at Piedra Labradas have two holes that were used to hold burning incense when honoring the gods. Other holes feature engraved serpents.

CONCORDIA

Concordia, 30 miles/45 km southeast of Mazatlan, is a mining village of 26,000 people known today for its ceramics and wood furniture. **San Sebastian Church**, located on the town plaza, was built between 1705 and 1785 and is the state's oldest church. Constructed of stone with a single tower, the building is still in perfect shape. The carved column at the other end features St. Barbara, Lady of Guadeloupe (the patron saint of Mexico) and St. Sebastian, the protector of the village. Across from the church is the sacristy with a sculpture of a man and his son (both missing their heads).

A **giant rocking chair** in the square makes one look like an elf when sitting in it. If you are here on January 20, you will be able to partake in the town's greatest **festival**, which celebrates liberation from the French.

QUEST FOR RICHES

Basque national Francisco de Ibarra came looking for silver and settled in Concordia, then called San Sebastian. He never did find the rich mother lode, but he did establish Concordia and Copala, a bit farther east. He died in Panuco, at the bottom of a canyon, in 1575. In the 1800s, a German traveler called Alexander von Humboldt wrote about the 500 mines he found in Mexico that were rich in precious metals. Among the towns he mentions are Concordia, Panuco and Copala.

COPALA

Copala is 14 miles/21 km east of Concordia, and just 10 minutes walking off the main highway. The village can be reached by public buses (get off on the corner and walk the last section) or by your own vehicle. The town, a colonial silver-mining village with white houses topped in red clay tiles, was founded in 1565. Today it has 650 residences, narrow cobblestone streets, a quaint **plaza** with an austere **church** just a block away. The church is dedicated to St. Joseph and has one tower. The numerous plaques on the outside of the church could take an entire afternoon to read. If you decide to stay here, **Daniel's Hotel** costs $30 a night for two people. Daniels also has a restaurant that serves banana cream pie that comes highly recommended. There's also the **Copala Butter Company**, a café. I don't know anything about it, but the name alone is intriguing.

The **Tequila Factory** at **Hacienda Las Moras** is six miles/10 km past La Noria and along the same road. You'll need your own transportation to get here. The 150 year-old former tequila distilling plant has been converted, in part, to a restaurant. There are few of the old factory workings left, but many people come to gawk at

the rich environs and have a beer and lunch before heading on. Others stay awhile, whether there is tequila available or not. The factory is part of a guest ranch located on 2,000 acres that has a pool, chapel, tennis courts and horses for rent. There are reports that claim the horses are not well cared for here. You will have to judge for yourself. If you can see their ribs or if their hoofs are split, do not ride them. The grounds are home to birds, including peacocks, which roam freely through the rich vegetation. Note that you will not be allowed into the grounds unless you give advance notice. There are 11 villas, decorated in old Spanish hacienda style, but with modern bathrooms and air conditioning. The villas cost $280 for two, per night, including all meals. To tour or stay at the factory, contact them in Mazatlan at *Cocoteros #1, Rincond de las Palmas, in Zona Dorada,* ☎ *669-914-1346, www.lasmoras.com/english.htm.*

▨ AGUACALIENTE

Before Rosario, along the highway, is the village of Aguacaliente. It has numerous little **hot pools** that have curative powers, but they are used mostly for washing clothes. However, the hot springs are not the draw to this town. Rather, the **piñatas** made here are the attraction. If you are at all artistic and would like to know how to make one of these items specific to Mexico, see if you can join a class.

PIÑATAS

Piñatas were originally used by the Franciscan Fathers to portray the idea of the devil hiding treasures of goodness. The Franciscans made the piñatas of papier mâché in the shape of the seven-pointed star with each point representing one of the seven deadly sins. Cumulatively, they symbolized the devil. The treats inside represented good and the resistance to sin. The mythical idea was that if you hit the devil hard enough, he would release all the good things he held. Today, the piñata has developed into every shape and size possible and is usually full of candy that falls onto the floor when the piñata is broken. During Semana Santa, some Mexicans make a Judas and fill him with firecrackers that are ignited. This results in Judas exploding, much to the delight of the watchers.

ROSARIO

The colonial village of Rosario is 47 miles/65 km from Mazatlan on the way to Tepic. First established in the mid-1600s, it now has a population of about 75,000.

> **LOCAL LINGO:** *The town name comes from a legend. A herdsman was coming home after finding a lost cow. He was playing with the beads of his rosary and, just before dark, the beads broke. Not wanting to lose them, he made a fire to cook some dinner and then spent the night so that he could look for the beads in the morning. Instead, he found a very rich vein of silver, smelted out of the ground by his fire.*

Our Lady of the Rosary Church is the main attraction in town. The golden baroque altar dates from the 18th century. Of the statues, the Virgin of the Rosary is the most distinguished. There are wooden sculptures of saints around her. This church had to be moved from its original site because silver mining tunnels below it were causing structural damage.

The **Lola Beltran Museum**, on the street of the same name, is located in a house that was originally the family home. Born in 1932 in the village, Beltran was called the Queen of Mexican Ranchera music. She appeared in over 50 movies and recorded over 100 music albums. Lola started her career by singing in the church – it must have been the gold of the altar that inspired her. It was her teacher, Señor Gallardo, who encouraged her to sing elsewhere. She started to perform with mariachi groups; her popularity was, in part, due to the subject of her songs, which told of the downtrodden Mexican and the hardships he suffered. She became a world-renowned singer, and performed for people such as Eisenhower, Nixon, De Gaulle and Haile Selassie. Lola Beltran died of a stroke in 1996 and her body was laid to rest in Rosario.

OUTFITTERS/TOUR OPERATORS

Vista Tours, *Av Camaron Sabado, # 2 and 3,* ☎ *669-986-8610, www.vistatours.com.mx,* is in the Zona Dorada. They offer numerous day tours, such as the Tequila Tour or a trip to La Rosario. Both include lunch and cost $35 and $45 per person, respectively. They also offer a sight-seeing dinner tour, an afternoon Copala tour, or will take you on an all-day excursion into the jungles of San Blas for less than $100, including breakfast and lunch. Most of these tours include transportation, beer, water and soft drinks.

Marlin Tours, ☎ *669-913-5301, www.toursinmazatlan. com,* offers an excellent city tour that everyone should do at least once. City tours always give visitors a much better insight into an area not visited before. They will take you through Zona Dorada and the Aquarium, then go downtown and visit city hall, the cathedral and the lo-cal market. In the old town you get to visit the art school, the Angela Peralta theater and museum, as well as a number of historic houses. Also on the tour are El Mirador, where the cliff divers plunge into the sea, Look-out Hill and the lighthouse. This 3½-hour tour costs a mere $20, well worth every penny. Marlin does other tours too, like trips to Rosario, Teacapán and the Tequila Factory. The open-air, street car-styled trolley that you see around town belongs to Marlin.

Pronatours, *Av Camaron Sabalo in El Cid commercial area,* ☎ *669-913-3333, pronatours@mazatlan.com.mx,* of-fers tours to the Marine Turtle Hatchery. The hatchery is sponsored, in part, by El Cid. They also have bird-watch-ing excursions, Deer Island kayak and snorkel tours, mountain bike trips and whale-watching boats. They raise money to support the environment by selling t-shirts, arts and crafts, books and calendars. Although prices are unavailable for the tours mentioned above, their yacht rentals are $35 an hour or $210 a day for up to four people. Larger ones cost up to $450 a day for up to six people. This includes tackle, ice, insurance, captain and crew. Transfer from the airport to the city is $25 for up to four people.

Viajes El Sabalo, *Rodolfo Loaiza #200,* ☎ *669-914-3009,* offers a half-day catamaran trip to Adventure Island, where you can snorkel, ride horses, kayak, windsurf, or ride a banana boat or Jet Ski. The boat has music, an open bar, bathrooms and a sundeck. As you travel, keep an eye out for seals and other marine life. Viajes El Sabalo also have city tours, tours to Copala and Concordia, booze cruises and deep-sea fishing tours. Their costs are comparative to those of others operators.

SHOPPING

Prices are fixed in stores and galleries. However, in the market you can barter; about 25% discount should be expected unless the starting price is outrageous. In that case, just walk away.

Joyeria El Delfin, *Edificio Balboa, Av Camaron Sabalo #1600,* ☎ *669-914-3209, www.isabelmatiella.com,* carries jewelry designed by world renowned Isabel Matiella, who incorporates Mexican petroglyphs into her work. If you would like a special souvenir of the highest quality, consider one of these pieces.

Shell pendant by Isabel Matiella.

Madonna's, *Av Las Garzas and Laguna,* ☎ *669-914-2389, or Playa Gaviota #401,* ☎ *669-913-1467, www.madonnajewelry. com,* has an extensive selection of pottery and blown glass pieces at reasonable prices. These include Huichol Indian art, Mayolica ceramics and Talavera art, all made by Mexican artists. These are high-quality, intricately-designed products. You can get copies (of lesser quality and at lower prices) in the market in the old town.

Talavera candleholder.

Sea Shell City, *Calle Rodolfo Loaiza between Las Garzas and Av del Mar,* ☎ *669-913-1301, open 9 am to 8 pm,* has some of the rarest specimens of shells found in the Pacific, but it also has some of the tackiest shell-covered pieces in Mazatlan. This is where to shop if you want to get even with your mother-in-law.

Constantino's Leather Factory, *Av Camaron Sabalo, #1530,* ☎ *669-914-6434, and Av Playa Gaviotas #425,* ☎ *669-916-5550,* has high-quality leather goods, from jackets and pants to cowboy hats.

Gallery Michael, *Av Las Garzas #18, no phone,* is open Monday to Saturday, 9am-9 pm, Sunday until 4 pm. They have a huge selection of items from Tlaquepaque art centers in Guadalajara. Credit cards are not accepted here.

Pardo Jewelry, *Av Playa Gaviotas # 411,* ☎ *669-914-3354,* offers mostly bracelets, necklaces and rings that feature diamonds.

>> **AUTHOR TIP:** *Diamonds in Mexico are tax-free, so if you need that engagement ring or a present for mom, this is where to look.*

NidArt Galeria, *Av Libertad and Carnaval,* ☎ *669-981-0002, next to the Angela Peralta Theater,* is open Monday through Saturday, 10 am-2 pm. It specializes in masks, faces and sculptures of leather. The pieces for sale are all made by local artists, many of whom have studied in Mazatlan. If you want something different, stop by.

Mercado Central is in the center of town, near the cathedral. The market is full of tiny stalls selling everything from meat to t-shirts. Originally, this was a bullring but it was purchased in 1895 so it could be used as a marketplace. The prices aren't that much lower than in the shops and I found the quality to be average, rather than exceptional.

PLACES TO STAY

Like most tourist cities, Mazatlan has a plethora of hotels from which to choose. I can't possibly mention them all (60 are registered with the tourist office), so I have profiled only a few in the pages that follow. There should be something to suit every taste and budget.

HOTEL PRICE SCALE
Price for a room given in US $.
$. . . . . .Up to $20
$$. . . . . $21-$50
$$$. . . . . $51-$100
$$$$ . . . . $101-$150
$$$$$ . . . . $151-$200

HOTEL SAVVY

Never book the room for your entire vacation unless the deal is too good to ignore. Should the hotel you book with turn out to be a roach-infested dive, you then have the option of moving on. Also, you may not want to spend the entire time in the city, but instead head into the hills and explore. Always leave your options open.

Santa Maria, *Calle Rio Panuco, ☎ 669-982-2308, $,* on the main street across from the bus station, is the best of the three in the area. Each room has two beds, private bathroom, air conditioning and hot water. The owners are friendly and the prices do not change from summer to winter.

Hotel del Rio, *Av Benito San Suarez, no phone, $,* has some very tiny rooms that cost $12 for a double bed. The rooms with air conditioning for $18 are much better, although you couldn't hold a party in them. The hotel is exceptionally clean and the staff is friendly. There's an area where you can store some of your things when out on trips.

Hotel Bel Mar, *Olas Altas, no phone, $$.* This was the first hotel ever built in Mazatlan and the old doors at the entrance certainly attest to this fact. The original area still has its old tiles and some wall paintings, but is now used as the car park. The newer section was built around a pool and all rooms have air conditioning. The place is a bit battered, but the charm makes up for it and the service is exceptional. It is also on the beach and in Old Mazatlan. Hotel Bel Mar was originally built in the 1920s by Louis Bradbury, an American mining entrepreneur. He filled the back garden with exotic plants from around the world; the restaurant was notorious for its fine cuisine throughout the northwest. Two scandals occurred at the hotel.

SCANDALS AT HOTEL BEL MAR

In 1922, General Abelardo Rodriguez's wife committed suicide in one of the rooms. He later became president of Mexico. A second scandal occurred during Carnival in 1944, when State Governor Rodolfo T. Loaiza was murdered in his room after attending the Queen's ball. Today, the place seems *tranquilo.* At least, I came out of it alive.

Hotel La Siesta, *Blvd Olas Altas #11,* ☎ *669-981-2334, www.lasiesta.com.mx, $$,* has rooms around an open central courtyard that is adorned with ancient trees. The

rooms all have air conditioning and TV, and are clean and well kept. The cost is $35 for a double without a view of the ocean and $47 for a room with a view. This is one of the best deals in town if you go for old and charming. The on-site Shrimp Bucket Restaurant, opened in the 1950s, was so successful that it was the start of what is now a fairly large chain around Mexico.

Hotel Plaza Gaviotas, *Rodolfo Loaiza,* ☎ *669-913-4322, www.plazagaviotas. com, $$,* across from Playa Mazatlan, has 67 rooms with air conditioning, telephones, cable TV

PLACES TO STAY

1. Santa Maria
2. Hotel del Rio
3. Hotel Bel Mar
4. Hotel La Siesta
5. Hotel Plaza Gaviotas
6. Royal Dutch B&B
7. Playa Mazatlan
8. Royal Villas
9. Posada Freeman
10. Las Flores
11. Aguamarina Hotel
12. Costa de Oro
13. El Quijote Inn
14. Holiday Inn
15. Hotel Plaza Marina
16. Los Sábalos Resort
17. Pueblo Bonito Resort
18. El Cid

PLACES TO EAT

19. El Parral
20. El Marismeño
21. Shrimp Bucket
22. Restaurant Bar del Pacifico
23. Machado, Pedro & Lola
24. Señor Frogs
25. Panama
26. Señor Pepper
27. Vittore Italian Grill, Joe's
    Oyster Bar
28. Casa Loma
29. No Name Café
30. Valentino's Disco,
    Bora Bora Bar
31. Ambrosia Vegetariano
32. VIP
33. Angelos
34. Soho
35. Club Mia
36. Mundo Bananas
37. La Taberna
38. Tony's Bar & Grill
39. Bahai Mariscos
40. Fiesta Mexicana

1 MILE

1 KM

and private bathrooms. Parking is available. The hotel is across the road from the beach. There is a bar and the Green Chile Restaurant on site. When I was here, the restaurant was a popular place for Mexican families. I interpret this as a sign that the Mexican food is good.

Royal Dutch B&B, *Calle Juarez #1307 and Av Constitution,* ☎ *669-981-4396, $$$,* has two rooms at present and they have plans for two more in the near future. The cost is $65, including a huge breakfast of almost anything you could want. Often, tea and goodies are offered at night. Rooms are in a restored house in the old section of town. This place is run by a Dutch man married to a Mexican woman, who operate a clean and comfortable establishment. If you are into the quiet and small, try them. Royal Dutch is closed every summer from June to October.

Playa Mazatlan, *Rodolfo Loaiza #202, www. playamazatlan.com.mx, $$$,* has over 400 rooms on five floors and the reports I have seen make this one of the better places to stay in this price range. The service is excellent, the Mexican hacienda-style hotel is exceptionally clean. From the front-facing rooms that are now being remodeled, the surf can be heard hitting the seawall. There is a pool, a fitness center, laundry service, childcare, parking, a restaurant and a snack bar on site. Each room has a hair dryer, cable TV, iron, coffee maker, data port, alarm clock and air conditioning.

Royal Villas, *Av Camaron Sabalo #500,* ☎ *669-916-6161, www.royalvillas.com.mx/, $$$,* has large, well-decorated rooms with tiled floors and private balconies. Many overlook the ocean. The suites all have fully equipped kitchenettes and eating areas, and the deluxe rooms are big enough for eight people, with two bathrooms and two balconies. There is air conditioning, parking, a purified water system, laundry service, satellite TV, wheelchair access, a money exchange, safe deposit boxes and a business center. This large hotel is right on the beach. The rate for the penthouse, which holds six people, is less than $100 per person, per night. Before booking, be sure to ask about special promotions. La Hacienda de la Flor restaurant at Royal Villas is one of the best in town.

Posada Freeman, *Av Olas Altas #79,* ☎ *669-981-2114, $$$,* is an old classic built in 1944 and named after the designer Guillermo Freeman. It was Mazatlan's first sky-scraper. The hotel was closed in 1985 due to lack of business, but has since been purchased and remodeled by Best Western. It has become a popular spot in the old city. It has 64 rooms, done in typical Best Western style, with coffee maker (coffee included) and an Internet connection in the rooms. Breakfast is included in the price. There is a rooftop swimming pool that is very attractive.

Aguamarina Hotel, *Av Del Mar # 110,* ☎ *669-981-7080 or 800-537-8483 (US), www.aguamarina.com, $$$/$$$$,*

© Aguamarina Hotel

has smallish rooms and larger suites complete with kitchenettes. The hotel is small and not right on the beach (you must walk across the *malecón),* but it has a nice pool and is clean. Rooms have tiled floors, private bathrooms, air conditioning, satellite TV and telephones. This is a popular place with Mexican people. There is a restaurant and bar.

Costa de Oro, *Av Camaron Sabalo #710,* ☎ *669-913-2005, www.costaoro.com, $$$/$$$$,* is an older hotel, right on the beach, with 180 rooms and 110 suites. Rates are often discounted for promotional purposes. Rooms have double beds, air conditioning, satellite TV, bathrooms and phones. Suites have all of the above, plus a kitchenette and balcony. There are three tennis courts, a snack bar, two restaurants, two bars, safe deposit boxes, a travel agency, car rental and shopping on site. There is also laundry service and free parking.

© Costa de Oro

Las Flores, ☎ *800-452-0627 (US), 877-756-7529 (Canada), www.lasflores.com.mx/english/indexENG.htm, $$$/$$$$*, is a small hotel with just over a hundred suites, studios or standard rooms. Suites can hold up to six people and have fully equipped kitchenettes; studios and standard rooms hold up to four people. The rooms have tiled floors, beamed ceilings, air conditioning, sitting areas and cable TV. Located with a view out to Deer Island, the beach has gentle waves. Las Rejas bar here is famous for its happy hour.

El Quijote Inn, *Av Camaron Sabalo and Tiburon,* ☎ *669-914-1134 or 800-699-7700, www.elquijoteinn.com, $$$/$$$$*, has Mexican décor throughout. The 67 clean rooms have cable TV, private bathrooms, comfortable beds, equipped kitchenettes and sitting areas. There is a pool with very cold water, a Jacuzzi, business center, parking area, beauty salon, bar and lounge, safe deposit boxes and tennis courts. This is a safe place where the staff gives green gringos assistance and good advice. The hotel is on the beach.

© Plaza Marina Hotel

Hotel Plaza Marina, *Av Del Mar #73,* ☎ *669-982-3622 or 800-711-95465, www.hotelplazamarina. com, $$$/$$$$*, has over 100 rooms and suites, all of which are a fair size. Although not elaborate in their décor, they do have balconies, air conditioning, cable TV and private bathrooms. The pool is at the back of the hotel, rather than at the front facing the beach. The palapa huts on the beach are serviced by the hotel's waiters.

Holiday Inn, *Av Camaron Sabalo #696,* ☎ *669-913-2222 or 800-716-9707, www.holiday-inn.com, $$$/$$$$*, has 183 rooms that have recently been remodeled. Each room has air conditioning, kitchenette, satellite TV, telephone, radio, fridge, hair dryer and tiled bathroom. The hotel is on the beach and has private palapa huts for guests. There is an indoor and outdoor pool, a tennis court, a racquetball court, babysitting service, a playground, and a restaurant and bar. All the reports I have say that staying here is a great deal for the money.

Los Sábalos Resort, *Av Playa Gaviotas #100,* ☎ *669-983-5333 or 800-528-8760 (US), 877-756-7532 (Canada), www.lossabalos.com, $$$$,* is a five-star, Mediterranean-style hotel located on Las Gaviotas beach. It has 200 rooms and suites, some with ocean views, all with balconies. Suites and standard rooms have one or two queen-sized beds, satellite TV, telephones, tiled bathrooms, coffee makers, hair dryers, safe deposit boxes and air conditioning. An all-inclusive deal runs $100 per person, per day, double occupancy, and includes all meals. The hotel has a spa, steam room, sauna, Jacuzzi, massage room and beauty parlor. The treatments offered include a facial ($38), manicure ($11), pedicure ($15), full body waxing ($22) and body peeling ($38). For the peeling, I hope the knife is sharp. There are five restaurants on site that go from the casual Joe's Oyster Bar to the elegant Vittore Italian Grill.

Pueblo Bonito Resort, *Av Camaron Sabalo #2121,* ☎ *669-914-3700, www.pueblobonito-mazatlan.com, $$$$/$$$$$,* has 247 suites that are tastefully decorated with the sitting area separated from the sleeping area by arches. The tiled floors add a coolness to the breeze coming in off the ocean. Each suite has 575 square feet that gives you ample room for a long-term vacation. Each kitchenette is fully supplied with a fridge, stovetop, coffee maker, toaster, microwave and dishes. The dining areas seat four. There are ceiling fans and air conditioning, telephones, satellite TV, hair dryers in the bathrooms, private safes and irons and ironing boards. The hotel has parking, daily maid service, laundry service, bilingual staff, a tour office, auto rental, currency exchange and baby sitting service. The hotel is wheelchair-accessible. Rooms hold four or six people (two kids) and cost between $165 and $300 per night. The Royal and Presidential suites run more than double that. The hotel is on the beach and tucked into the bay, beside a nice rock outcrop.

El Cid, *Av Camaron Sabalo,* ☎ *669-913-3333 or 800-525-1925 (US), www.elcid.com, $$$$/$$$$$ (high season up* *to $680 per room)*, is four hotels and a shopping center rolled into one city within a city and is so distinct that it has become a landmark. It is one of the largest resorts in Latin America and has a fully equipped marina and sail-ing fleet, 27-hole golf course, squash, racquetball and tennis courts (instruction is available), spa, fitness facilities, tour desk and dive shop. The tennis courts have ball machines, video analysis and rental rackets. You can get lessons and clinics that run from a half-day to four days from November to May. The hotel has 1,086 rooms, eight swimming pools, eight restaurants, three bars and a private beach. Each room has a balcony, private bathroom, satellite TV, air conditioning, ceiling fans and telephone.

© El Cid Hotels

ISLA DE LA PIEDRA

Hilton Estrella del Mar, *Isla de la Piedra*, ☎ *669-982-3300, www.estrelladelmar.com, $$$$$*, is a hotel and resort community with condos for sale. The compound has 3.5 miles/six km of private beach and an 18-hole golf course designed by Robert Trent Jones, Jr. Hotel accommodations include air conditioning, hand-carved wooden furniture, and either ocean or garden views. The hotel has a formal restaurant and a bar, swimming pool, Jacuzzi, volleyball courts and beach palapas. There is also a commercial area and ambulance service to Sharp Hospital in Mazatlan or "Life Flight" to the US.

RV PARKS

There are six RV parks in the Mazatlan area. Prices run $20 to $25, depending on services.

San Fernando Trailer Park, *Av Tiburon*, ☎ *669-914-0173*, has 57 sites with water, electricity, sewers, bathroom facilities, laundry, pool, cable TV, telephone, green areas, mail service, social center and Jacuzzi.

Mar-A-Villas, *Av Sabalo Cerritos,* ☎ *669-984-0400,* has 35 units with water, full bathrooms and a social club. The park is on the beach.

La Posta, *Av Rafael Buelna #7, Laguna del Camaron,* ☎ *669-983-5310, www.mazatlan.com.mx/servicesand advice/trailerparks.htm,* has 180 sites with water, electricity, sewers, barbeque pits and cement pads. The park has full bathrooms, laundry, pool, telephone, green areas, mail service, ice, purified water and a social club.

San Bartolo, *Av del Pulpos,* ☎ *669-913-5755,* has 48 sites with water, electricity, sewers, barbeque pits and cement pads. The park has full bathrooms, laundry, cable TV, telephones, green areas, mail service, a social center and a Jacuzzi.

Mar Rosa Park, *Av Camaron Sabalo #702,* ☎ *669-913-6187,* has 82 sites with water, electricity, sewer hookup and cement pads. The park has full bathrooms, cable TV, telephones, green areas, mail service, a social center and purified water. The park is located on the beach.

Las Palmas, *Av Camaron Sabalo #333,* ☎ *669-913-5311,* has 66 sites with water, electricity, sewer hookup and barbeque pits. The park has full bathrooms, a pool, cable TV, telephones, a money exchange office, green areas, mail service and a social center.

PLACES TO EAT

There are so many restaurants in Mazatlan that I could not possibly eat enough in a year to try them all. I have taken recommendations from others to add to my own personal list. Most meals in average restaurants cost around $10 per person. Coffee shops are much cheaper and the fine dining places cost $15 to $20 per serving. Some portions are very small, most are average, and a few eateries offer a decent-size plate.

El Parral, *on the* malecón *next to Hotel Amigo,* ☎ *669-990-1368,* may be okay for some things, but I was charged US $8 for a small jug of lemonade. It wasn't listed on the menu so the waiter charged about three times the price in other cafés. My mistake was not confirming the price before ordering.

Restaurant El Marismeño, *Olas Altas #1224 on the* malecón, ☎ *669-912-2612,* has okay coffee and exceptionally good cheese omelets served with fried potatoes. The French toast is coated with sugar and cinnamon so, if this is not to your liking, let them know. Their specialty, as with many restaurants here, is seafood. This restaurant uses its own boats to bring in the fish to ensure freshness. It is usually excellent.

Shrimp Bucket, *Av Olas Altas #11-126,* ☎ *669-981-8019, open 7 am-11 pm,* has a decent breakfast, but the coffee leaves a lot to be desired. However, their specialty is dinner, notably shrimp. They have things like *camarones escabeche* (pickled shrimp), *ensalada atun* (direct translation is nitwit salad, but it really means tuna salad), *empanadas* (pastry filled with seafood), *pescada* Veracruz (fish in a tomato sauce) and *sopa verde* (green soup). Servings run $5-$10. The first Shrimp Bucket was opened on this site in the 1950s and its popularity grew so that it is now a leading Mexican chain.

Restaurant Bar del Pacifico, *Av Del Mar #1910,* ☎ *669-981-3150*, is along the *malecón* on the far side from the beach. It serves some of the best food in Mazatlan for around $8 a plate. I had fish done in a special Mexican hot sauce. The waiter was attentive, but not hovering, and the drinks were not watered down. I suggest you try this restaurant at least once.

Ambrosia Vegetarian Restaurant, *Sixto Osuna #26,* ☎ *669-985-0333,* is open 7 am-10 pm, with specials offered at each meal. The prices are excellent, the service good, the food delicious.

La Taberna D. Miguel, *Av Camaron Sabalo,* ☎ *669-916-5628,* open 5-10 pm. This taco bar is great for a drink and tacos or a quesadilla. Costs are $1 for a small beer, $3 for a tequila and $4.50 for the special that includes a glass of wine or a beer, re-fried beans, a sausage, tortilla and salad.

Machado Restaurant and Bar, *on Machado Square in the old town,* open 8 am-11 pm, is a great place to sit and watch life pass by. It offers good seafood and live music on weekends.

VIP's, *Camaron Sabalo and Albatroses,* ☎ *669-914-0754,* has air conditioning and a magazine store attached. For English-language readers, I saw *Time, Newsweek, Scientific American* and *Reader's Digest* for sale. This is an American chain, so the food is American chain food – frozen fries, cheap buns, tinned soup and ketchup. At least it's familiar. You can get a good burger here.

Pedro and Lola, *Constitución and Carnaval on Machado Square,* ☎ *669-982-2589,* has street-side tables. The food is excellent, as it is at the other four restaurants on the square.

Restaurant Casa Loma, *Av Gaviotas #104,* ☎ *669-913-5398,* is open daily from 1:30-10:30 pm. They opened their doors in 1976 and offer a quiet Mexican (oxymoron?) atmosphere for those who like out-of-the-way places. The food is international and the prices are around $15 for a meal.

Joe's Oyster Bar, *Av Playa Gaviotas #100,* ☎ *669-983-5333, www.lossabalos.com,* is open 11 am-2 am and is located in Los Sabalos Resort. Joe's is a fun place on the beach, and their specialty is fresh oysters and shrimp tacos served with exotic drinks. If you are not into exotic, have a beer. It is also an open-air disco.

Vittore Italian Grill, *Av Playa Gaviotas #100,* ☎ *669-986-2424, www.lossabalos.com*, is open noon-1 am and is in Los Sabalos Resort on Las Gaviotas beach. This is an exquisite restaurant, complete with white linens and black-jacket waiters. Their pizzas are baked in a wood-fired oven, the pastas are homemade fresh every day and the desserts are made by an Italian cook. They also serve lamb chops, a rarity in Mexico. Most of the wines are imported.

Tony's Bar and Grill, *Av Rodolfo Loaiza and Camaron Sabalo,* ☎ *669-983-5700,* has the mix of great burgers and live music.

Angelos, *Av Camaron Sabalo # 2121 at the Pueblo Bonito Hotel*, ☎ *669-914-3700,* open 6-11:30 pm, is a quiet piano bar decorated with polished wood and crystal chandeliers. The best gourmet dinners include shrimp, pasta and scampi that should be enjoyed with a good bottle of imported wine. The wine selection is large. The average cost of a meal is $15. There is a dress code; beachwear, jeans and flip-flops are not permitted.

No Name Café, *Av Playa Gaviotas #417,* ☎ *669-913-2031,* is open for meals from noon to 12:30 am. This sports bar has good barbeque ribs, although the steaks are not the best in town. They also serve pork chops, hamburgers and barbequed chicken that is very tasty. Happy hour runs from 5-6 pm and again from 10-11 pm. Watch the "happy hour" prices, as they are often higher than the regular prices. No Name is also open for breakfast at 8 am. The sports section has 30 large-screen TVs and two giant screens, and is decorated with tons of posters, pennants, photos and baseball cards.

Señor Pepper, *Av Camaron Sabalo,* ☎ *669-914-0101,* open 5 pm-midnight, is located across from Hotel Playa Real. The attached bar is open 5 pm-2 am. This eatery belongs to the same chain as the Shrimp Bucket – a company that knows what the average Jill and Joe want. Their specialty is prime rib steak or lobster (in season) for about $25. All meals are served under candlelight in an elegant setting with potted plants and polished crystal. There is live entertainment and dancing.

Pura Vida, *Bugambilia #100 and Laguna,* ☎ *669-916-5815,* is open 8 am-10 pm and offers decent-sized servings. For breakfast, you can get coffee, juice, whole-wheat pancakes or omelets. Lunch has soy burgers, vegetarian pasta dishes or sandwiches – all are excellent. Soups are recommended. Prices never exceed $7 per person.

Jungle Juice, *Av de las Garzas,* ☎ *669-913-3315,* open 8 am-10 pm, is located on an open terrace. The music is loud but the atmosphere is appealing. I love the name. They specialize in grilled meats and juice and smoothies. It was the smoothies that gave them their reputation. They also have some very good vegetarian dishes.

Bahai Mariscos, *Av Mariano Escobedo #203*, ☎ *669-981-2645,* open 10 am-8 pm, has the best fried fish in town. They also serve their famous seafood stew. Meals are average in price and size. The restaurant is located in a restored old house; the owner will take you on a tour. This restaurant was opened in 1950 by Alejandro Flores Curlango; his specialty was ceviche. If you are stopping here for an afternoon beer, try a ceviche snack.

Soho, *Av Camaron Sabalo #312,* ☎ *669-913-1300,* is a traditional sushi bar that serves other Japanese foods, including their specialty, Yakimeshi (a fried rice dish that has ham, onion, ginger, sesame oil, eggs, dashi sauce, sugar and pepper).

Panama, *Calle Dominguez and Sixto Osuna,* ☎ *669-981-7517,* is another popular chain where you can get mostly Mexican dishes, but also things like a ham and cheese sandwich or a cheeseburger for $3. Their fresh juices are excellent and their milkshakes (*liquido de fruta con leche*) are not to be missed. They cost under $2 for a large glass. Panama is also a pastry shop. If you need some cake and coffee, this is the place to stop. It is always busy, an indication that the food is good.

NIGHTLIFE

Mazatlan is known as the party city, so finding action after sunset is no problem. The city is safe, so having a drink or two should not hamper your personal safety. However, do not get loaded and then stagger down a dark alley with all your money in your back pocket (or your front one, for that matter). It is also best if you travel in a group after being at the bar, because a person alone is an easy target.

Valentinos is set in this unusual building.

Valentinos Disco, *Punta Camaron,* ☎ *669- 984-1666,* is the huge Moorish-looking structure that can be seen a long way down the beach. It is a definite draw for the young. There is a $5-$10 cover charge. The light show here is 21st century in style and sound. To get away from the modern disco, you can have a game or two of pool in the next room. The **Bora Bora** bar, also in this building, has a volleyball court and a surfing simulator.

Cuba Mia, *Av Camaron Sabalo, #406,* ☎ *669-913-9692,* is open Tuesday through Sunday, 5 pm-2 am. This is a lively Cuban bar with Cuban music and dancing, and Cuban foods. They also offer special events, for which you must purchase tickets.

Señor Frogs, *Av del Mar,* ☎ *669-982-1925, www. senorfrogs.com/mazatlan,* is one of the most popular discos in town. The locals come here to mingle with party-addicted tourists. Drinks are fairly reasonable in price and the music is loud and modern. The most popular drink is the *coscorrones* (tequila shooter). There are rumors that some rowdy guests have danced on the tables late into the night. If you would like to eat while here, I recommend the ribs. Señor Frogs usually has good security and well functioning air conditioning.

A FROG OF MANY COLORS

Señor Frogs is one of those strange Mexican franchises that you find everywhere and in every form – it can be a clothing store, a disco or a restaurant.

Mundo Bananas, *Av Camaron Sabalo #131,* ☎ *669-986-4700,* is a catch-all with clothes, pool tables and a bar. That should just about cover all the needs of any customers.

Fiesta Mexicana, *Hotel Playa Mazatlan,* ☎ *669-913-5320,* has traditional food along with a folkloric music and dance show. The meal is gourmet Mexican buffet, consisting of things like pineapple tamales, enchiladas with fresh cheese and smoked marlin tostadas. They serve unlimited domestic drinks. Shows run every Tuesday to Saturday from 7 pm to about 10:30 pm. The music comes from four states in Mexico and the dancing is exuberant, the costumes exquisite. They do things like the Fire and Machete dance, magic shows, a comedy act and the Mexican hat dance. The cost is $28 per person and $14 for children under 11. This is a professional show and a must to see at least once.

Mazatlan

North of Mazatlan

Guasave

This attractive little city of 100,000 people is just 25 miles/50 km from the ocean. Located on the Sinaloa River, the town supports an agricultural population, one that grows corn, wheat, sor-

ghum, soy, cotton and beans. The biggest draw for visitors are the Nio Ruins, which date back 800 years, and the birdlife on the islands at Las Glorias.

SERVICES

Contact the **Police** at ☎ *687-872-1232.*

There's a **medical center** on *Av Lopez Mateos #643,* ☎ *687-872-8283.*

SIGHTSEEING

The **Church of the Rosary** near the plaza has a statue of Mary with the Christ child in one arm and a rosary dangling from the other. The statue is paraded through town on the first Sunday every October and the last Sunday every November. The church itself is not overly ornate.

ADVENTURES ON WATER

Playa Las Glorias is known for its sunsets and its abundant bird population. To get to Tamazula and Las

Glorias, south of Guasave, follow the signs and the paved highway for six miles/10 km to Cubelete. Turn south (left) and follow the road for 4.5 miles/eight km to Tamazula. Take the dirt road across from the church in Tamazula and follow it past Zerote and Brecha. Las Glorias is eight miles/13 km past Brecha.

> ▶▶ **BIRD WATCH:** *There are Swainson's hawks, forest falcons, finches, verdins, terns and pelicans. Those with a bit more birding knowledge should keep an eye out for colima warblers, blue, black and gray gnat-catchers, laughing gulls, ring-billed gulls, Hermann's gulls, herring gulls and snowy egrets.*

Just south of Las Glorias is a 50-mile/80-km bay dotted with islands and inlets. Both the Mocorito and Evora rivers drain into this stretch of water, creating a rich estuary. The most important areas for birding are **Red Beach Bay** and the **Bay of Santa Maria the Reformation**. The islands of interest are **Saliaca**, **Altamura** and **Tachichilte**. The island of Altamura is especially interesting because of its large sand dunes. You will need to hire a boat to take you out. The fishing villages of La Reforma or Las Glorias have people who will rent you a barge. Ask around. Besides Mr Moro's Place on the beach just south of Las Glorias, the villages of Guasave, Angostua and Navolato have comfortable places to stay and numerous places to eat. Angostura and Navolato are along Highway 15 (also referred to as the main or interstate highway) heading south toward Mazatlan.

Navachiste Bay is a long bay (one mile/two km) that is part of a 30-mile/50-km stretch of inlets and islands. Just south of that stretch there is a peninsula and another 50 miles/80 km of the same. The entire shore has white sand interspersed with rocks. The area is enjoyed mostly by birds and a few Mexican fishermen. The bay is protected by the islands of San Ignacio and Macapule (15 miles/23 km long and two miles/2.5 km wide) to its north and is dotted with mangroves (where rivers drain into the ocean) that house numerous varieties of birds. White storks and plovers are the most common birds in the area. Inland, mountains rise at least 600 feet/200 meters and those that reach the shore often stop abruptly, leaving high cliffs.

The islands south of Navachiste Bay are filled with wildlife and some have ancient rock sculptures. All are good for photographers. One of the islands is called the **Island of the Poets**. It got its name when an international group came here every year to write poems. The landscape offers inspiration for literary creations. Another island is called **White Hill**, because of the guano that sparkles against the red rock. **The Windows** is another island where rocks have been used for recording history. Some of the petroglyphs represent sea creatures and are fairly large, standing up to three feet/one meter.

Bird Island is a must for birders. Surrounded by mangrove swamps and dotted with spiny underbrush, it is a haven for feathered friends. To find a boat to take you to the islands, stop by Mr. Moro's Place at the hotel/RV site in Las Glorias.

White stork.

▶▶ **BIRD WATCH:** *Bird Island has cormorants, storks, pelicans, seagulls, frigates and osprey. Farther inland you will find ibis, storks, vultures, and numerous songbirds. Even during non-migratory periods, birds abound. Records show that 117 species live on this island.*

Fishing is good at the mouth of Sinaloa River, but the rocks are steep and take a bit of clamoring around before you find a good perch.

ADVENTURES IN CULTURE

Nio Ruins archeological site is less than six miles/10 km west of town on Sinaloa River. There are also a number of old missions farther up the river. Nio has a necropolis that was in use between 800 and 1,200 years ago. At that time, this farming community made ceramics that were superior to those of other villages. Found at the site were burial jars, plates, bowls and pots. The ceramics indicate to archeologists that residents traded with people as far away as Oaxaca and Mexico City. One of the vases, made of alabaster, is similar to some found in the Veracruz area. Once the Jesuits arrived, they converted people to Catholicism and built structures in the European fashion. Walls and two complete arched entrances from the early Jesuit missions still stand. The mud brick buildings that served as the monastery and church are also in fairly good condition. Only one of the buildings has a roof on it.

Tamazula is 11 miles/18 km south of Guasave and is the last mission town along the river. The mission was founded by Father Clerecis. It was built in the 16th century but was later destroyed by cyclones. The present church was built in 1820 in the Franciscan style. The museum attached to the church shows religious artifacts. The route to the mission is also a good way to reach Las Glorias Beach, one of the best along the coast. To get to the mission, turn off Highway 15 at El Cubilete and follow the signs to Tamazula. To get to Playa Las Glorias, follow the dirt road opposite the church.

PLACES TO STAY

San Enrique Motel, *Blas Valenzuela #42*, ☎ *687-872-0040, $$,* has 48 rooms with private bathrooms. Free parking.

HOTEL PRICE SCALE	
Price for a room given in US $.	
$. . . . . .Up to $20	
$$. . . . . $21-$50	
$$$. . . . . $51-$100	
$$$$ . . . . $101-$150	
$$$$$ . . . . $151-$200	

Hotel Mission, *at Km. 144 on Highway 15, no phone, $,* prefers to rent rooms by the hour. It is very basic but includes porno flicks.

Trebel Park Hotel, *Km 153 Carretera Nogales,* ☎ *687-872-8395, $$,* has 40 rooms with all the basic amenities plus a secure place to park.

Hotel del Rosario, *Corregidora #150,* ☎ *687-872-0003, $$,* is a three-star hotel with 30 rooms, all with private bathrooms and air conditioning.

Mr Moro Hotel and RV Park, *Blvd El Tiburon #1000,* ☎ *687-873-7007, www.mrmoro.com.mx, $$$,* has 20 rooms and 80 RV sites right on the beach at Las Glorias. The rooms have air conditioning, great views, private bathrooms and comfortable beds. Rooms are clean and pleasantly decorated. There is a pool surrounded by palapa huts and a children's play ground. The RV sites all have full hookup. A restaurant on site serves international and local dishes with specialties like shrimp, calamari, onion rings and salads. The bar makes excellent margaritas. Mr Moro also rents boats with guides so you can fish or visit the islands.

Hotel El Sembrador, *V. Guerrero and Emiliano Zapata,* ☎ *687-872-4011, www.hotelelsembrador.cjb.net/, $$$,* has 85 rooms and 10 suites. All have air conditioning, carpets, cable TV, private bathrooms, purified water and soft beds. There is laundry service, a money exchange, a travel agent and free parking. A restaurant, bar and disco are also on site. The disco has music every night but the bar has it only on the weekends. The restaurant has a breakfast buffet on Friday, Saturday and Sunday that is popular.

North of Mazatlan

PLACES TO EAT

Retaurante El Granero, *V. Guerrero and Emiliano Zapata*, ☎ *687-872-4011, www.hotelelsembrador.cjb.net,* in the Sembrador Hotel is about the best place to have a meal unless you head out to the beaches and eat seafood from one of the palapa huts.

Restaurant La Pizzeta, *Blvd Central #115,* ☎ *687-872-7777,* has pizza for reasonable prices. This is always a safe bet.

South of Mazatlan

The coastal road between Mazatlan and PV is mostly undeveloped. The tiny villages along the way such as Concordia (page 130) and Rosario (page 133) are worth a visit just because they are so calm and Mexican. For the botanist or ornithologist, Teacapán is a must. If you have your own vehicle, the possible stops are innumerable. If traveling by bus, staying in Tepic and doing day/overnight trips is a good option.

Tepic

Tepic has all the conveniences of a big city coupled with the friendliness of small-town Mexico. I love the people, who always had time to tell me a story or show me something. The tourist office was so enthusiastic about my visit they gave me a list of the special places in the area and got me to report back on them. The food was delicious, and the hotel I stayed in was exceptionally comfortable. The city is dotted with beautiful parks and squares and the main town square is always bustling with events. If you are in this region and not staying in the ocean towns, then stay in Tepic.

GETTING HERE

BY PLANE

Amado Nervo Airport is about eight miles/12 km from the center of town and out past the bus station. It is named after the famous poet Amado Nervo, who was born in Tepic. I do not know of any other airport anywhere that is named after a poet. Serviced by Aero California, Mexicana and AeroMexico, it has flights from Mexico City, an hour away, and from Tijuana on the US border, about 2½ hours away. From here, you can fly to Puerto Vallarta and connect to other places from there.

AIRLINE CONTACT INFORMATION	
Aero California	☎ 800-237-6225 (Mx) www.aerocalifornia.de
AeroMexico	☎ 800-237-6639 (US); 800-021-4010 (Mx) www.aeromexico.com
Mexicana	☎ 800-531-7921 (US); 800-509-8960 (Mx) www.mexicana.com

BY BUS

It is a pleasant half-hour walk on Calle Insurgentes from the central plaza to the bus station. A cab will cost $2. The station is serviced by **Elite**, **Omnibus**, **Futura**, **Transportes del Pacifico**, **Norte de Sonora** and **TuriStar**. There are restaurants and a cafeteria at the bus station.

BY CAR

The main highway that goes through Tepic is Highway 15, which follows the coast all the way to the Guatemalan border to the south and the US border to the north. It is a four-lane toll road that is well marked with huge signs.

HISTORY

The first settlements in the area were at **Matanchen Bay** about 5,000 years ago. Around 350 to 650 AD, people started moving inland. Under Toltec influence they developed crops using terraces reinforced with fabric made from vegetable fibers. Between 700 and 1200 they began making ceramics, jewelry and stone and metal figurines. They also built the great ceremonial centers.

Tepic has been a center for trade and commerce all through the 16th and 17th centuries and now is the center of government for the state of **Nayarit**. Although most of the area's historical events took place at San Blas, it was **Nuño Beltran de Guzman** in 1532 who started commerce in the area. At the same time the adventurous **Jesuits** went inland to spread the word. After they were expelled, the people of Tepic started planting tobacco and citrus fruits that grew well in the shadow of the two volcanoes, **Ceboruco** and **Sanganguey**. They soon realized that the volcanic soil, heavy rains and altitude of 8,500 feet/2,500 meters made the area good for grain, sugarcane, cotton and coffee.

The state of Nayarit was part of Guadalajara and the state of Jalisco, but turbulence led Nayarit to separate in 1884. It finally became a state in 1917, with Tepic as the capital.

▶▶ **LOCAL LINGO:** *The name Tepic comes from the Nahuatle Indian words "Tetle," that means rock and "Pic" that means hard. Together the word is Tetlepic, which has eventually changed into the easier pronunciation, Tepic. Originally the Spanish called the town Santiago de Compostela, but the more popular Indian name stuck.*

TEPIC'S CITY SEAL

The final version of the seal was completed in 1993. It has seven human footprints that symbolize the seven Nahuatl tribes that formed the Aztec nation. The central part of the shield has the right side profile of an eagle devouring a snake. The eagle stands for strength of the sun and the snake for value of the earth. The seal can be seen at the regional museum in the center of the city.

SERVICES

Post office, *Calle Durango #33 between Allende and Morelos, Monday to Friday, 8 am-6 pm, and until noon on Saturday.*

Hospital, *Paseo de la Loma, next to La Loma Park,* ☎ *311-213-7937.*

The **Police Station**, *Tecnologica #3200,* ☎ *311-211-5851,* is a long way from the center.

The **Tourist Office**, *on the corner of Puebla and Nuervo just past the Presidential Palace,* is one of the most helpful tourist offices in all of Mexico. Since most of them are exceptionally good, that says a lot.

SIGHTSEEING

Amado Nervo Museum, *Zacatecas # 284 North,* ☎ *311-212-2916, hours unavailable,* is located in the house where this famous poet was born on August 27, 1870. He schooled in Tepic until he was 14 and then worked on the newspaper in Mazatlan. He then went to Paris, where he worked on *El Imparcial* newspaper and met Ana Cecilia Luisa Daillez, the love of his life. By the time he returned to Mexico he was quite well known. Nervo died on May 24, 1919. Inside the house are numerous documents, many of the furnishings as they were when he lived here, photos of his wife and daughter and the big wooden desk where he wrote. The house became a museum in 1967. You can buy books of Nervo's poems here, but English translations are not available.

Quatro Pueblos Museum, *Hidalgo #60 West,* ☎ *311-212-1705, Monday to Friday, 9 am-7 pm (siesta 2-4 pm).* The property, an 18th-century colonial house, was made into a museum in 1992, with the five rooms dedicated to the local indigenous groups of the area. The first room has costumes and artwork of the Huicholes, including the intricate beadwork for which they are so well known. The second has artwork of the Coras, Tepehuanas and the Mexicaneras groups. This includes wall hangings and pictures. The third and fourth rooms have work from the

Tepic, Ixtlan, Jomulco and Mexpan villages. All of these villages are located in the mountains and the work is very different. The final room has work from the Pacific Ocean. Mostly this covers fishing implements and tools for building palapa huts.

Anthropological and Historical Museum, *Av Mexico #91 North, ☎ 311-212-1900, 9 am-6 pm*, is inside a colonial building built in the mid-1800s by Felipe Liñan. In the last century, the German Consulate was housed here. It left in 1933 and the state school of Fernando Montaño operated in the building until 1948. It became a museum in 1949, originally displaying classical and neo-classical archeological items. In 1969 it expanded to include the bones of prehistoric animals found in the area. There is a permanent collection of ceramics (many of which feature tropical fruits) from the western cultures of the country. On the upper level is a huge crocodile from the San Blas area. It is more than 12 feet/four meters long. One room is dedicated to religious colonial art.

Museum of Juan Escutia, *Hidalgo #71 West, ☎ 311-212-3390, Monday-Friday, 9 am-1 pm and 5-7 pm,* is in yet another 18th-century colonial house. Juan Escutia was one of the child heros of Chapultepec, the area in Mexico City where children held the Americans at bay for four days. It was in 1846 when Mexico declared war on the US and on September 11th of the same year, US General Scott attacked the Fort of Chapultepec that was defended by 632 soldiers from the Battalion of San Blas and 200 young cadets. As the battle raged, all the soldiers were killed. Eventually, the US Army entered the fort and, while still defending their land, five young cadets died. One was Juan Escutia. Juan's parents, José and Maria Martinez, lived here until 1869. Inside you will find the birth certificate of Juan, along with pictures of other Chapultepec heros. There are military uniforms and pictures of Juan as a cadet, along with the flag of San Blas and medals from that era. Juan Escutia was born in Tepic on February 22, 1827 and joined the military in 1847. When he was at battle in Chapultepec, he was the bearer of the flag.

Museum Aramara (Museum of Visual Arts), *Av Allende #329, ☎ 311-216-4246, Monday-Friday, 9 am-1 pm and 5-7 pm,* has two rooms with permanent exhibits that feature paintings done by local artists. The six inside rooms have modern art, photographs and plastic arts. The late 18th-century colonial building was first a school and, later, the only sanatorium in the state.

Museum of Emilia Ortiz, *Av Ledro #192, ☎ 311-212-2652, Monday-Friday, 9 am-1 pm and 5-7 pm,* has a permanent exhibition of this talented artist's work. She is not only an excellent painter, but also a poet and a journalist who received recognition from peers in those fields. Born in 1917, Ortiz has been an artist for over 70 years. The museum is well lit, with benches on which to sit and admire the works.

The Plaza has the Palacio de Gobierno, built in the 1800s, facing the 18th-century Cathedral of the Pure Conception of Mary and the 16th-century Temple of the  Cross of Zacate. The temple originally was a Franciscan convent but today is home of the State Ministry of Tourism. The center of the plaza has a lovely fountain and there is always some type of event happening nearby.

A City Tour is offered free of charge by the town of Tepic. You must get your ticket an hour before the bus leaves from the kiosk on the plaza in front of the cathedral on Av Mexico and Amado Nervo. Even during off-season, this is a popular tour. It starts at 10 am and ends at 5 pm, and is conducted in Spanish only. The historical tour includes some of the parks and old buildings. The vehicle looks like a remodeled milk truck with rows of seats, but no doors. Being open air, visibility is good. This is an excellent opportunity to see Tepic.

ADVENTURES ON FOOT

Volcán Ceboruco is 8,000 feet/2,164 meters high. You can drive all the way to the crater during dry season. While on the highway, you will see remnants of the last eruption that took place in 1870, killing everyone in the surrounding villages. Previous eruptions occurred in 1567 and 1542. To get here, take a bus from Tepic to Jala, a colonial village at the foot of the mountain with less than 500 residents. Purchase all your drinking water and food here, as there is nothing available farther along.

> **FACT FILE:** *This area is credited with growing the longest ears of corn in the world, some of which reach up to 19 inches/48 cm.*

The Gothic-Romanesque-styled **Lateran Basilica** built in the 18th century is worth visiting while in the village. The old church (not the basilica on the plaza, but up from it) dates back to the 1500s. You can climb the bell tower for a look at the town. This old church, built in the typical Spanish style with white plaster and a bell tower to one side, once also served the convent next door. There is a **museum** in town, near the plaza, that has some maps, statues and ancient animal bones.

Stay at **Hospedaje Camberos**, *on Av Hidalgo, $,* if you want to spend the entire day on the mountain and are too late to get back to Tepic or if you just want to spend a day in this tiny Mexican village. The lady in the store next door will open the door for you with a key that looks like it should be for a prison rather than a home. There are two very clean bathrooms for the five tiny, basic rooms in the *hospedaje*. Each room has a bed with mattress and sheets. The two recommended restaurants in Jala are **Joya** and **Don Miguel**, both on Dom Conocido.

From Jala on the southern slope, walk along the cobblestone roadway that leads up the mountain toward the microwave towers. As you get near the top it becomes obvious that there are actually two craters, one beside the other. Near the rims of these are the microwave towers.

South of Mazatlan

From the towers you can follow a path toward the center and then to the top of the bigger cone. Steam still leaks up from underground, which means you should be careful where you plant your foot. One of the craters has a flat floor and numerous pine trees. This is a good picnic spot. There's also another picnic area that can be driven to. You will need hiking boots (runners won't do), water, warm jacket, food and sunblock to explore the volcano area.

This is a magnificent hike. However, if you are the driving kind, you can get near the top with a vehicle.

ADVENTURES ON WATER

Aguamilpa, a man-made lake, is 4.5 miles/seven km from Santa Maria del Oro. The 55,000-acre lake was created by damming Mexico's longest river, the Santiago, for the Aguamilpa Hydro Electric Power Plant. The 70-mile/ 100-km lake is surrounded by vegetated hills that pour scenic waterfalls into its waters. It is also a fishing lake where stocked bass is the draw. One lakeside lodge caters to anglers. **Aguamilpa Lodge**, *Bass Adventures,* ☎ *505-377-2372 (US), PO Box 995, Angel Fire, NM, 87710, $$$$$,* has 16 rooms and sits on a cliff overlooking the lake. An all-inclusive package available between November and April includes lodging, meals, drinks, boats and guides.

Mexcaltitlan is the Venice of Mexico because the streets of the town flood every rainy season. Located at the mouth of a river in a large lagoon, Mexcaltitlan is an island that is believed to be where the Aztecs first left to go inland and start the city of Tenochtitlan, now Mexico City.

The small, round island is in a swamp/mangrove area and can be reached by hired boat, available at the dock (see directions below). The island's one village has one hotel and restaurants that specialize in making pre-Hispanic foods. There is a museum that holds the thousand-year-old stone carved with the eagle devouring a serpent.

The museum also has arti-
facts from the indigenous
people who lived here thousands of years ago. Buses
from Tepic bus station go every two hours. You go first to
Santiago, then on to
Santispac. The road gets
rough between Santispac
and Mexcaltitlan. At the water, there is a dock where
you can hire a boat to take
you to the island. The cost is
less than $5 round trip.

If traveling in your own vehicle, leave it at the boat landing but lock it up and take
all valuables.

Mexcaltitlan, flooded.

ADVENTURES IN NATURE

Centro de Educacion Ambiental (Environmental Education Center), ☎ *311-212-9409,* is five miles/eight km
from town, just 10 minutes by taxi. It is open 8 am-1 pm
daily; admission is $1. This educational center promotes
conservation, appreciation and investigation of the out-
doors. Located on 26,000 hectares of forest, the center
offers an extensive amount of flora and fauna for the
public to enjoy. Swing bridges cross delicate canyon areas that feature every type of plant imaginable. With the
lush jungle comes the numerous bird species that can be
observed from special platforms. Because the jungle has
gone back to its natural state, the temperature is always
around 20°C/68°F and the humidity is high. An interpre-
tive trail has 18 labeled points of interest and the main
center has an audio visual show (in Spanish). Take with
you insect repellent, a hat, binoculars (essential) and
hiking boots or good runners. It will take about three
hours to make the tour.

Laguna de Santa Maria del Oro is 30 miles/50 km
southeast of Tepic and five miles/eight km from the town

of Santa Maria del Oro. This crater lake measures one mile/two km wide and is surrounded by hills covered in pines and subtropical vegetation. Birding is the favorite activity, but people also come to swim or fish in the lake. Stocked with bass and tilapia, the lake yields fish weighing up to six lb/2.5 kg. Small restaurants around the lake serve the specialty called *chicharron de pescado* (fish sausage). Although motorboats have not been banned from the lake, Jet Skis have, a real plus for the eco side.

There are some lakeside cabins with private bathrooms, hot water and kitchenettes at the **Bungalows Koala**, ☎ *311-212-3772* (phone in Tepic because there are no phones at the lake). Tucked into bougainvilleas and snake plants, they are well kept and have potted plants decorating the brick buildings. There is also a restaurant. Those with RVs or tents can camp here. The bungalows are owned by Chris French and his wife, who first came to the area 20 years ago because they liked the name. They could have done better business moving to the coast, but they liked the climate of the lake and decided to stay. They are into preserving the environment and encourage the use of non-motorized transportation. This is truly a gem of a place.

The roads around the lake are barely rough tracks and hikers, bikers or horseback riders can spot the birds mentioned below and maybe find some new plant life not seen before in Mexico. It takes two hours to walk around the lake at a leisurely speed. You can purchase juice, water or a beer from one of the lakeshore restaurants.

▸▸ **BIRD WATCH:** *Birds at the lake include grebes, pelicans, cormorants, herons, hummingbirds, trogons, ducks, motmots, kingfishers, neotropical creepers, vultures, ospreys, hawks, flycatchers, chachalacas, sandpipers, swallows, kingbirds, cotingas, swallows, crows, jays, pigeons, doves, parrots, wrens, cuckoos, owls, thrushes, gnatcatchers, mockingbirds, woodpeckers and finches.*

The church in Santa Maria del Oro village has a statue donated by Nuño Beltran (known to the people of the village as "Bloody" Guzman) in restitution for the murders he committed while trying to conquer the area.

The restaurants in town are **La Parroquia**, near the church, and **La Cocina Economica**, in front of the square. I have no information about these places.

ADVENTURES IN CULTURE

Los Toriles de Ixtlan del Rio is an archeological site about 60 miles/88 km from Tepic. Buses to Ixtlan leave every hour from Tepic and Guadalajara. At the village you can hire a taxi to take you to the ruins just one mile/ two km west.

This is not a huge ruin, but it is unique because it has the only circular Maya temple found to date that is not an observatory. Occupied by the Tumbas de Tiro group around 300 BC-600 AD, the area covered approximately 200 acres. After the Tumbas de Tiro fell, the Aztatlan people occupied the town.

Ceramics found at the site were unique to the Chinesco, Ixtlan and San Sebastian areas. They featured predominantly red, orange, yellow and cream colors and the subjects were mainly women, war, work and music. The later ceramics made by the Aztatlan group were of smooth red clay. Found in the homes of the common people were earthenware pots and red tripod grinding mortars.

The later group of inhabitants perfected the use of metals and worked the metal into jewelry with intricate designs. They also used a lot of obsidian that was probably transported from Volcano Ceboruco, not far from Ixtlan. The obsidian was carved on both sides.

South of Mazatlan

At the site, pit tombs were found. This method of burial is believed to have been practiced until 600 AD when the Aztatlan people took over. There is also evidence of stairways, drainage ditches, small residences, workshops, altars and palaces. Of course, the most impressive ruin at the site is the round temple called Ehecatl-quetzalcoatl. The two circular tiers have steps leading to the top where there are two pyramids. Adjoined to the circular tiers is the Palace of the Bas Relief and, in front of it, the main square with the Palace of the Columns flanking one side.

The site is open every day from 9 am until 5 pm. The information center has pamphlets from the National Institute of Anthropology and History. There are also bathrooms and a picnic area. Rumors have it that there will be a tourist lodge in the future.

There are numerous hotels in Ixtlan village and most are in the middle price range. The Plaza Hidalgo offers the most luxurious services, but it is not necessarily the best. Look around and compare to see what suits you best. The hotels mentioned below are recommended by the tourist office in Tepic. Most are along Av Hidalgo. **Hotel Colon**, *Hidalgo #359, 311-243-3919, $*, has 32 basic rooms. **Hotel Santa Rita**, *Hidalgo #125,* ☎ *311-243-2451, $*, is a tiny place with just a few basic rooms. It was originally called The Maya. **El Paraiso**, *Hidalgo #757,* ☎ *311-243-2000, $$*, has 20 rooms. **Plaza Hidalgo**, *Hidalgo and 5 de Mayo,* ☎ *311-243-2101, $$$,* is a four-star hotel with 42 rooms equipped with everything you need.

There are about 20 restaurants, including the **Three Gold Stars**, **Happy Chicken**, **Moby Dick** and **Fisherman**. Like everything else, most are on Av Hidalgo. If they look clean and serve what you want, give them a try.

PLACES TO STAY

Hotels are spread around the city. There are numerous two- and one-star options beyond the plaza toward Av Victoria and then more west of the plaza but also toward Victoria.

Hotel Cibrian, *Amado Nervo #163, 311-212-8699, $,* has moderately large rooms with private bathrooms and tiled floors. The place is clean and the staff is friendly. It is the only decent and moderately priced hotel that is close to the square and it is my choice.

HOTEL PRICE SCALE
Price for a room given in US $.
$. . . . . .Up to $20
$$. . . . . $21-$50
$$$. . . . . $51-$100
$$$$ . . . . $101-$150
$$$$$ . . . . $151-$200

Villa Las Rosas, *Av Insurgentes # 100,* ☎ *311-213-1800, $$,* is across from the Hill Park and zoo. It has two floors with 30 rooms built around a courtyard. Each rather plain room has cable TV, air conditioning, tiled floors, private bathroom with hot water and ceiling fan. Parking is on site. The price of the room includes a continental breakfast in the Handrails Restaurant (7 am-10:30 pm). At night you can dance at the Faisan Disco, also on the premises, where the weekend begins on Thursday.

Sierra de Alica Hotel, *Av Mexico #180,* ☎ *311-212-0322, $$,* is half a block from the square and patronized mostly by Mexican businessmen. It offers laundry service, pharmacy, beauty salon, money exchange, safe deposit boxes, a travel agent and off-street parking. I did not find the hotel staff friendly, although those in the restaurant were. It is open at 7:30 am and serves excellent meals.

Hotel Las Palomas, *Av Insurgentes 2100,* ☎ *311-214-0238 or 800-713-8500, www.laspalomashotel.com.mx, $$$,* is fairly nice. It overlooks a busy street so rooms at the back are recom-
mended. Each room has a private bathroom, cable TV, air conditioning, telephone and a sitting area. There are reading lights over the beds, the floors are tiled and there are large closets for your stuff. There is a restaurant, bar and parking.

Hotel La Loma, *Paseo de la Loma #301,* ☎ *311-213-2222, $$$,* is close to the park and zoo. This comfortable place has lush gardens surrounding a small pool. Rooms are clean and well furnished with cable TV, tiled bathrooms, ceramic floors, cupboards and night lights. Each room also has a sitting area with a small table. The staff is pleasant, the grounds well kept and the price is reasonable. There is a restaurant, bar and parking. La Loma is close to many good restaurants, although it is about a 10-minute walk to the plaza.

Hotel Melanie, *Blvd Tepic Xalisco #109,* ☎ *311-216-1888, $$$,* is a half-hour walk or a five-minute cab ride from the center of town. Its 43 rooms are set around a clean vegetated courtyard that has tile walkways. Unfortunately, the tile reverberates sound and makes it a bit noisy during times like carnival. There is air conditioning, cable TV, daily maid service, restaurant and laundry service.

Hotel Fray Junipero Serra, *Lerdo #23,* ☎ *311-212-2525, www.frayjunipero.com.mx, $$$,* is on the plaza. It has over 100 spacious rooms with air conditioning, carpets, private bathrooms, cable TV, telephones and safe deposit boxes. There is laundry service, pool and a restaurant that's popular with locals. This is a good deal.

Hotel Real de Don Juan, *Av Mexico and Juarez,* ☎ *311-212-1324, $$$,* is across from the Government Building, just off the plaza. The rooms are large, with queen-sized beds, private bathrooms, night tables and tables beside the windows where you can sit and watch the action on the street (if you are at the front). There is also a restaurant and bar.

Nekie (Fiesta Tepic) Hotel, *Av Insurgentes and Lago Victor,* ☎ *311-207-0768, $$$$,* has a 1940s atmosphere, but the place has been modernized to provide air conditioning, tiled floors, safe deposit boxes and cable TV.Its 240 big rooms have high ceilings. There is an outdoor pool, laundry service, parking, restaurant, beauty parlor, bar and gift shops. This is a five-star hotel with five-star service.

PLACES TO EAT

There are a few dishes traditional to the province of Nayarit. **Pescado Sarandeado** is grilled fish cooked over mangrove wood. This dish may no longer be available since mangroves are now being preserved. **Pate de camaron** is a shrimp pâté and **taxtihuili** is a corn broth that has shrimp cooked into it. If you see any of these dishes offered, be certain to try them.

> ▶▶ **AUTHOR NOTE:** *Most of the better restaurants are away from the plaza and on or near Av Insurgentes.*

Sierra Hotel Restaurant, *Av Mexico #180,* ☎ *311-212-0322*, is a tiny place with a cozy atmosphere. The food is excellent and inexpensive. I had the chicken for $3.50 and the portion was big enough to fill me. What really impressed me here was the staff. They went out of their way to make me welcome and to give me everything I wanted. Then they turned around and let a beggar kid in to have something to eat.

Cheros, *Av Insurgentes #233, across from Alameda Park, no phone*, specializes in *banarilla*, an interesting dish of chopped barbeque pork or beef mixed with spices. A T-bone or New York steak costs $7.50. The meat I tasted had a smoked flavor and was tender. This is a popular place for those in a hurry who like a grilled meat dish. It's open 7 am-2 am daily.

La Mision de Trinos, *Hidalgo # 73,* ☎ *311-212-2180*, is a very clean place in the center of town that serves excellent food. Their *liquidos* are thick and their *huevos rancheros* (eggs with tomato and onion) are good. They serve international foods, so getting a sandwich or a good plate of chicken is easy. Prices are about $4 per meal.

Alta Mirano, *Av Mexico # 105 South,* ☎ *311-212-1377*, is above the square beside the cathedral. You must enter the building and go to the back stairs and then up. The food is good, although not exceptional. The view is what you really pay for. They are open early, so breakfast is popular here. The coffee is good and the service reasonable.

Mariscos Lalo's, *Calle Allende and Ures,* ☎ *311-216-4421*, is popular for seafood. There is a take-out service and the lines are always long.

El Girasol, *Paseo de la Loma # 201,* ☎ *311-213-4293,* is close to La Loma Hotel and is a vegetarian restaurant. The food is excellent, considering this is a meat-eating nation. There are lots of salads.

Fu Seng, *Insurgentes # 1199,* ☎ *311-214-5988*, is beyond Alameda Park and is a stark room with tin tables and plastic chairs. However, the stir-fried vegetables are excellent, and the prices are low.

NIGHTLIFE

Fundacion Nayarit, *Lerdo de Tejada #57,* ☎ *311-216-4064,* is the art center of the city. It opens at 10 am and, depending on the function, doesn't usually close until late. During the day you can have a cappuccino and a piece of cheesecake and enjoy the bohemian ambiance. There is original art on the walls and a small bookstore that sells local poetry books, many of which are self-published. A calendar of events lets you know what is happening that month. Most events start at 8:30 pm and have a cover charge of about $1.50 per person. Offerings include things like "*Musica Romantica* by Los Sobrinos" and "Luis Lucachin Reading Ballads of Yesterday and Today." For me, this place was a real treat.

Teacapán

To get to the village of Teacapan, travel about 57 km south on Highway 15 to Esquinapa. Follow the signs to Teacapan. The road comes to a T, at which point you should go right, cross some railway tracks and continue for another 40 km to the village.

The reason to visit Teacapan is the huge estuary formed where the Cañas River enters the ocean, forming a *marismas* or salt marsh that houses numerous bird and salt-resistant plant species. Besides the natural beauty of the bay, the area is *muy tranquilo* – very peaceful.

PLACES TO STAY

In the village there is **Hotel Denisse**, *Calle Morelos and R. Buelna, right on the square,* ☎ *695-954-5266, $$,* that has only six rooms around a courtyard dotted with plants. The rooms have private bathrooms and air conditioning and the place is clean. For food, there are two places that are recommended; the **Playita** near the laguna and **Mr. Wayne's** in town. Both specialize in fried fish for about $5 per serving.

HOTEL PRICE SCALE	
Price for a room given in US $.	
$. . . . . .Up to $20	
$$. . . . . $21-$50	
$$$. . . . . $51-$100	
$$$$ . . . . $101-$150	
$$$$$ . . . . $151-$200	

Just out of town is the **Villas Maria Fernanda**, ☎ *695-953-1343 or 954-5393, www.villasmariafernanda.com, $$$,* that has an eco-lodge on the beach near the largest estuary in Mexico. The cabins, which can hold four or eight persons, are white-plaster buildings with palm-fond roofs, tiled floors inside and bamboo railings on the porch. The beds are soft and the place is clean. Cabins have an air-conditioning unit, TV, stove and fridge. Outside, the huge grounds contain a pool, hot tub and palapa huts for shade. There are thousands of palm trees, banana trees, bougainvillea and other colorful flowering trees on the property to help shade the environment that holds 55 species of tropical birds. There are also barbeque pits available for each residence and a children's playground. The hotel has kayaks and bikes for rent and they can arrange for horseback riding, snorkeling or deep sea diving. But mostly they take people on bird/plant tours of the wetlands. Kayaks cost $6.50 per hour and bicycles cost $3.50 an hour. Although they don't have horses on their property at the moment, there is some whispering that they will in the near future. There is English spoken at the villas and the owners are extremely friendly. This is a great place to stay.

Your final option is the **Rancho Los Angeles**, ☎ *665-953-2550, $$$,* which has 21 rooms in all with the best being in the main building rather than those facing the highway. The adjacent trailer park has room for 40 motor homes. There is a restaurant and pool on site.

San Blas

*T*he Bells of San Blas was written by Henry Wadsworth Longfellow. It was his last creation before he died on March 24, 1882.

> *What say the Bells of San Blas*
> *To the ships that southward pass*
> *From the harbor of Mazatlan*
> *To them it is nothing more*
> *Than the sound of surf on the shore,*
> *Nothing more to master or man.*
> *But to me, a dreamer of dreams*
> *To whom what is and what seems*
> *Are often one and the same,*
> *The Bells of San Bas to me*
> *Have a strange, wild melody,*
> *And are something more than a name*
> *For bells are the voice of the church*
> *They have tones that touch and search*
> *The hearts of young and old*
> *One sound to all yet each*
> *Lends a meaning to their speech*
> *And the meaning is manifold.*

This is the newest and, so far as I can tell, the most beautiful beach in all of Mexico. The 50 miles/80 km of sand and surf is dotted with a few estuaries and undisturbed by huge hotels. But that will change rapidly and my guess is that in 10 years my comments about the place and the hotels will be history. The town is a tiny fishing village of about 12,000 people and is surrounded by rain-forests and mangrove swamps. At present those stretches of beach hold surfing waves, ruins from the early Spanish explorers, turtle sanctuaries and wildlife-riddled estuaries.

▶▶ **AUTHOR NOTE:** *The only drawback to visiting San Blas are the* **mosquitoes** *and the insects referred to as a* **sand fleas**, *no-see-ums or jejenes (hay-HAY-nays). Avon's Skin so Soft is good for the jejenes and for your skin. Long shirt-sleeves and long pants are also a help. Insect repellent is a must. The reason there are so many insects is because there are mangrove swamps nearby. Don't let the insects stop you from coming; just come prepared.*

GETTING HERE

Buses from Puerto Vallarta cost about $12 and take 2½ hours on a first-class bus. San Blas is two hours by bus from Tepic and four from Guadalajara.

The closest **airports** are in Puerto Vallarta, Tepic and Guadalajara.

HISTORY

San Blas, founded in 1768, became an important port for the Spanish. It was **Manuel Rivero y Cordero** who, under command of Carlos II, made San Blas the port for Spanish ships sailing along the California coast. The Customs House was the first one built in the New World and served as both a tax collection place for incoming goods and as a defense fort. It was also from here that

Fray Junipero Serra.

Fray Junipero Serra, a Franciscan missionary, ruled the 15 missions along the coast. He arrived in San Blas on April 1, 1768 and, using two ships that had just been built in the harbor, started colonization of the area. Fray Junipero Serra died in San Carlos Barromeo de Carmelo on August 28, 1784.

MISSIONS ESTABLISHED BY SERRA

1769 – San Fernando de Velicata and San Diego de Alcala

1770 – San Carlos Barromeo de Carmelo

1771 – San Gabriel Arcangel and San Antonio de Padua

1772 – San Luis Obispo de Tolsa

1776 – San Juan Capistrano

1776 – San Francisco de Asis

1777 – Santa Clara de Asis

1782 – San Buenaventura

SERVICES

The **Tourist Office**, *Calle Mercado, Monday to Friday, 8:30 am-5 pm, Saturday until 1 pm*, has maps, a guide-book and pamphlets about the area. The staff speaks English and is quite helpful. They sell used paperbacks written in English.

Police, *Calle Sonola, across from the bus station,* ☎ *323-285-0028.*

People at the **Health Center**, *Calle Campeche and Batallion,* ☎ *323-285-0232*, speak only Spanish.

Post office, *Calle Sonora and Echeverria,* ☎ *323-285-0295, Monday to Friday, 8 am-2 pm.*

ADVENTURES ON FOOT

The Mafia Hotel is not a place you will want to stay, but it is interesting to walk around and have a look at what may have been had nature not intervened. The luxurious stone structure, located on the beach, has over 150 rooms overlooking the ocean. On the opening night, when even the president was there, an army of sand fleas (*jejenes*) attacked, sending the guests back to their homes in the city. Now the building is falling apart. Obviously, the owners had not heard of Skin so Soft by Avon – a sure-fire protection from the pesky biting bugs.

The Ruins, on Cerro de San Basilio at the northeast end of town above the cemetery, include the remains of La Nuestra Señora del Rosario Church and the Contadura, the counting house. The church was built in 1769 and was used until the late 1800s. The counting house was built with large stones and held together with little mortar. It had arched doorways. The old cannons around the building were used to keep British pirates away. During the 18th century, José Maria Mercado used this fortification to successfully keep invaders out.

> **FACT FILE:** *The first ship to arrive and be taxed here was the Chinese Nao coming from the East with silks and spices.*

Although restoration was being done at the ruins, a recent hurricane took out a lot of the work. There is a $1 entry fee. There is a bathroom at the gate. Open daily from 10 am to 6 pm.

The old **Customs House** is located across the river from the docks. It is constructed of brick that is now crumbling. Next to the ruins is a new, rather nondescript Customs House but it, too, is not in use.

Isla del Rey is on the bay and is actually part of the peninsula, rather than an island. It is the sacred lands of the Huichol Indians and has a pilgrimage trail. The Indians came to this site every spring to worship the sea goddess, Aramara. Today they still come, dressed in traditional costume, to enjoy their spring celebrations. You must cross the estuary by boat to get here (50¢). The dock is across from Tesoro Bungalows.

Cerro Vigia, near ceremonial grounds of Isla del Rey, holds El Faro, the red-and-white striped lighthouse where you can get good views of San Blas. A trail from the dock passes scrub and the Huichol ceremonial ground before heading up the hill. You must cross the estuary by boat to get here (50¢). The dock is across from Tesoro Bungalows.

ADVENTURES ON WATER

■ BEACHES

La Islitas Beach has the longest wave in the world, according to the Guinness Book of World Records. This wave is supposed to be about 20 feet long (six meters) and can carry the skilled surfer for a mile or more before petering out. The beach is five miles/eight km south of

San Blas and buses pass by every half-hour. There are a number of beachside restaurants, some with hammocks where you can relax, read and enjoy a beer. You can be certain there will be many experienced surfers talking the talk and waiting for the "Big One".

Borrengo Beach is about half a mile down (south) on the beach and is where those who are into camping hang out. The bugs can be bad, so repellent is essential. Intermediate surfing is good along this beach, but you must bring your own equipment. Boogie boards are also fun here. Snorkeling is not good because of the murky water.

▨ WATERFALLS

El Cora Waterfalls are 30 feet/10 meters high. They are located just out of the town of El Cora on an old hacienda that was once owned by Germans. The revolution of 1910-1914 resulted in the land being confiscated by the new rulers. Petroglyphs dot the trail. The walk is not long and there is a cool pool to swim in at the bottom of the falls. The tiny stream that forms the waterfall empties into the river below. It can be crossed below the pool and a grunt up the side of the cliff will take you to an-

other pool and falls. Take a bus (the white one) or drive from San Blas to El Cora town (10 miles/16 km) along the road to Santa Cruz/Tepic. Turn south at Tecuitata and go five miles/eight km to a loading platform where you can leave your vehicle. Follow the creek downstream. The final bit is steep, so hiking boots are recommended. Bring your bathing suit.

Tecuitata Waterfalls are near the village of the same name. Go the same way as to El Cora, only half a mile past the village of Santa Cruz get off the bus or turn downhill along a dirt road where the sign indicates Balneario Nuevo Chapultepec. At the bottom of the hill there is a waterslide, a restaurant and a small pool. Walk upstream through the jungle to the Arroyo Campsite and the waterfall. This waterfall is not as spectacular as El Cora, but certainly easier to reach.

ADVENTURES IN NATURE

■ BIRDING

According to the Audubon Society, San Blas is second only to Panama for having the largest number of bird species. There are many habitats – mangroves, mud flats, lagoons and offshore islands with thorn scrub and pine/oak woodlands – where you might spot rare and exotic birds.

▶▶ **BIRD WATCH:** *More common Mexican birds, like the blue bunting, the yellow-winged cacique and the mangrove cuckoo, will be easy to find. However, avid birders should keep a lookout for bare-throated tiger herons, lesser roadrunners, boat-billed herons, Colima pygmy-owls (these are so cute!), Rufous-necked wood-rails, rosy-thrush tanagers and military macaws.*

Military macaws.

Most birders log over 200 species in a week. If you don't have a bird book with you, purchase the one at the tourist office, *Where to Find Birds in San Blas*. This book tells you of other places around town where birds can be seen.

A spotting scope or binoculars is essential. Bring insect repellent.

 Where to Find Birds in San Blas, by Soalind Novick and Lan Sing Wu, is available by mail (178 Myrtle Court Arcata, CA 95521, US $4.50) or you can purchase it at one of the hotels/shops in town.

San Cristobal and **El Pozo Estuaries** are birder specialty places, but they are also rich with turtles, iguanas and crocodiles. The vegetation includes vines and giant ferns. Fresh springs run through the estuaries. The boat ride through this area goes for several miles, and San Cristobal estuary connects to the freshwater lake of La Tovara. The El Pazo inlet is where the annual fishing derby starts each year. Boats can be hired either at your hotel or at the dock. **Chencho**, ☎ *323-285-0716*, takes morning trips to San Cristobal and the cost, depending on duration, is $50 for up to five people. He takes you up the river to the lake. You need not go all the way if you are interested in seeing the wildlife in the estuary. This must be negotiated with the boatman.

La Tovara Lagoon is reached by traveling through the jungle and mangrove swamp up the estuary where crocodiles are wild and protected. Because there are so many, seeing them will almost become ho-hum by the end of the trip. However it is the Northern potoos, a bird that likes to be out after dark, that is the big draw. Green kingfishers and great black hawks are also common. Along the way you'll see vines, bromeliads, mangroves and flowering plants. At the right time of year, large hordes of butterflies gather here. An interesting spot on your river journey is an old movie set with huts on stilts set along the water's edge. The trip goes to a spring where you can swim in cool waters and then have a drink or a snack at the restaurant near the dock. The pool is large and the water clear. The spring provides drinking water for San Blas residents. There are fish in the water. **Chencho** (see above), the famous river guide, has an evening trip to the pool that costs $40 for up to four people. He is at the dock midday taking reservations and may group you with other people to make a load of four. You leave around 4 pm and return after dark. It is a thrill to travel through the jungle after dark. The sounds are eerie. Birders Novick and Wu suggest you hire **Oscar Partida**, who speaks English and knows his birds very well. He can be contacted by phone, ☎ 323-285-0324, or at Las Brisas Hotel.

You'll see crocs on your river trips in this area.

▶▶ **AUTHOR TIP:** *During peak seasons, when private boats are busy, the tourist office will put on a boat that is much cheaper than a private boat but also more crowded. See them at the office for details.*

Roca Elephante is a tiny island (a rock) just offshore to the northwest of the town that has both the blue- and brown-footed boobies as well as red-billed tropicbirds nesting. You will need to hire a boat at the dock to take you there. As you approach the island, swarms of frigate birds will cloud the skies. Peregrine falcons and pelicans also reside on Roca Elephante. You can't go onto the rock, but the boat will circle a number of times until you have had your visual fill.

Singayta Inlet is a jungle environment where El Manglar Environmental Center has built a traditional Nayarit village with a palapa hut that is used as an information center. Their objective is to protect the 260 species of birds in the surrounding forest. The organic nursery has prized orchids, some of which have taken four years to establish themselves. Near the huts are some Aztec petroglyphs. Boats are available to take people into the mangroves and lakes. To get here from San Blas, take the bus to Singayta (on the inlet and where El Manglar Environmental Center is located) from the plaza for a dollar each way. This is one of the most popular birding spots in all of western Mexico, even with the lush population of mosquitoes and sand fleas.

MEPG

The Mangrove Environmental Protection Group in San Blas was started in 1993 to protect the mangroves and surrounding land from mega-tourism and shrimp farms. Their main concern is education and enforcing the laws that have been passed. The president is Juan Garcia, a local businessman. Among other things, the group developed a bicycle path that leads from the entrance of town at Conchal Bridge, all the way to the bay and along the beach to Los Cocos. The most frequent users of this path are the oyster fishers.

Parque Nacional Isla Isabel is a bird and underwater sanctuary 52 miles/70 km from San Blas. It is a narrow volcanic island, one mile/1.6 km long that has a deciduous forest starting to cover the lava base. The island was formed about 3.5 million years ago and has evidence of nine separate volcanoes. There are bare rocks, cliffs and sandy beaches surrounding the small coral reefs just offshore. In the center is a crater lake with water 18 times saltier than the ocean. The landscape is unmatched and the island is often called the Galapagos of Mexico. It is

South of Mazatlan

also a birder's paradise, with numerous seabirds; blue-and brown-footed boobies nest here.

FACT FILE: *The interesting thing about boobies is the sibling rivalry. The oldest bird will often kill its nest-mates if food is scarce.*

There was at one time a huge colony of sooty terns on the island, but cats almost made them extinct. The cats were removed and the terns are recovering. Alongside the many endangered birds, Isla Isabel has a healthy community of amphibians, including the fake coral snake and the brown and green iguana. A research station operates for five months of every year, and visitors are welcome to camp as long as they bring all their supplies, including water. The researchers rely on local fishers and the navy to bring in water and supplies. **Ancla Tours** in Nuevo Vallarta, ☎ *322-297-1464*, takes people to the island. In San Blas, **Tony Aguayo**, ☎ *323-285-0364, at the end of Calle Juarez,* is a recommended guide. He charges about $200 per person (based on two people going) for a full-day island trip. His boat will hold about six people.

Cerro de San Juan Ecological Reserve, ☎ *311-213-1423,* is 6,200 feet/2,000 meters high and is another good hiking/birding area between San Blas and Tepic. It's about 15 miles/25 km from San Blas. The area has pine and oak forests.

▶▶ **BIRD WATCH:** *Rare birds have been spotted in the San Juan reserve, including Mexican wood nymphs and Rufous-crowned motmots. Although not seen, the eared-poorwills have been heard. There are also yellow grossbeaks, woodcreepers, red-starts and buntings.*

There is a ranch-style lodge at the top of the mountain. To get to the reserve, you must take a bus from the center of town. On the way you can stop at El Mirador del Aguila and look for military macaws.

■ CROCS

Ejido de la Palma Crocodile Farm is three miles/five km south of Matanchen Village, near Las Islitas Beach (see page 180). These crocs are in captivity. There is a freshwater lake on the site and the surrounding jungle houses butterflies, turtles and lizards. There is an entrance fee of $2 per person – the money goes toward the protection of the crocs.

OUTFITTERS/TOUR OPERATORS

Bird Treks, *115 Peach Bottom Village, Peach Bottom, PA,* ☎ *717-548-3303 (US), 800-224-5399 (Mx), www.bird treks.com,* offers a tour that starts in Puerto Vallarta. It takes half a day traveling to San Blas where you set up home base in one of the better hotels. The next seven nights are spent sleeping at the hotel, while the days are spent hunting birds with expert birders (who are also the tour leaders). The cost is $2,200 for an all-inclusive package from PV to San Blas and back. This does not include booze, personal supplies (such as mosquito repellent) or tips.

Wings Birding Tours, ☎ *888-293-6443, www. wingsbirds.com,* offers birding trips all over the world. I have worked with them in Bolivia and I know they are first class. Their website has a bird list that is far too long to put in here. The tour starts and ends in Puerto Vallarta, with most of the time spent in the San Blas area. This is a nine-day, eight-night tour that includes everything except the pen to tick off the birds seen. The cost is $2,450 per person for double occupancy. Wings allows only 12 people in a group, plus the leader.

PLACES TO STAY

Casa Morelos, *Calle Heroico Batallion # 108,* ☎ *323-285-0820, $,* is between town and the beach and two blocks from the bus station. The guesthouse has clean rooms without private bathrooms and is owned by the same family who owns **Casa Maria**, just around the corner (same phone number). Both have communal cooking areas and gardens in which to sit. These are friendly Mexican establishments that are comfortable but simple.

HOTEL PRICE SCALE
Price for a room given in US $.
$. . . . . .Up to $20
$$. . . . . $21-$50
$$$. . . . . $51-$100
$$$$ . . . . $101-$150
$$$$$ . . . . $151-$200

La Quinta California, *halfway between town and the beach,* ☎ *323-285-0603, $,* has bungalows around a common courtyard that is thickly vegetated with every plant imaginable, including a strangler fig tree. The rooms are not big, but the kitchens are fully equipped with small stove and fridge. Each comfortable two-bedroom bungalow has enough beds to accommodate four people. Prices are reasonable. However, you can get weekly and monthly rates that are even more attractive. There is no daily maid service.

Rafael's Apartments, *Calle Campeche and Calle Hidalgo, $$,* has clean apartments that surround an enclosed garden that is second only to La Quinta's. The kitchens have full stoves (ovens included). The place is clean, safe and economical, but there is no phone or e-mail address so you have to take your chances. Hit town and head over here.

Casa Roxanna, *Callejon el Rey #1, www.sanblasmexico. com/casaroxanna/, $$,* is a very neat and tidy little place that has a pool with an adjacent bar, and rooms with air conditioning, cupboards and cable TV. The kitchens are fully supplied with fridge and stove and have an apart-

© Casa Roxanna

ment-sized working area. The décor is tasteful, the floors tile. The sitting area is large and there is laundry service and secured parking. The large bungalows sleep up to five people and the small up to three. This is a real gem and, as a birder, I could stay here for a month with no problem. The gardens are lush.

Bungalows Conny, *Calle Chiapis #26,* ☎ *323-285-0986, www.bungalowsconny.sanblasmexico.com/contact.html, $$*, is a Mexican hacienda-style hotel that is comfortable and clean. The rooms have air conditioning, television, two double beds, private bathrooms and hot water. Laundry service is offered. This place is a good find and just four blocks from the main plaza.

Hotel Bucanero, *Av Juarez #75,* ☎ *323-285-0101, $$,* is older and with a décor that is more interesting than most in town. In the garden is an anchor and a couple of stuffed crocs. The rooms have high ceilings and are cool, but dingy. There is a pool, but no restaurant. Note that the disco next door could keep you awake on weekends.

Posada del Rey, *Av Campeche #10,* ☎ *323-285-0123, $$/$$$, www.sanblasmexico.com/posadadelrey.* Some of the dozen rooms have air conditioning, but none of the private bathrooms has separate shower stalls. There is a small pool with a poolside bar, a beach-supply shop and a restaurant. The owners are friendly and will arrange tours for you. They speak English, French and Spanish.

© Posada del Rey

Tesoro de San Blas, *Calle Campeche and Hidalgo,* ☎ *323-285-0537, www.geocities.com/dougcb68/tsb.htm, $$,* features rustic, three-room bungalows that have hot-water showers in the bathrooms, gas hot plates and refrigerators in the kitchens and a comfortable sitting space in the living rooms. The cabins are kept clean. There is a large maintained garden full of exotic plants like mango, banana and papaya. There is also off-street parking. One small room in the house is available for rent. The cabins are on the estuary so the view of the lighthouse adds to the sunsets. Birders like to use this as a home base because they can walk around the estuary when bird activity is high.

Hotel Hacienda Flamingos, *Calle Juarez # 105,* ☎ *323-285-0930 or 285-0485 (no English spoken), www.sanblas.com.mx, $$$*, is right in town close to the plaza. This is the restored German import house, first built in 1883 to receive goods from the orient. It was then called Casa Delius. The last officer to work at the Customs House was displaced in 1932 and had to find other work. His grandson purchased the building out of nostalgia in 1990 and started restoration that has been done to perfection. Photos of the family remain in the hallways that still have the original tiles. There is a pool, a fountain that works all the time and a lush garden. The eight rooms are as beautifully finished as the rest of the building and come with private bathrooms, air conditioning and coffee makers (coffee is supplied).

Hotel Garza Canela, *Calle Paredes # 106 South,* ☎ *323-285-0112, www.garzacanela.com/acommodations.htm, $$$*, has 45 large rooms with tiled floors, air conditioning and fans, satellite TV, safe deposit boxes and private bathrooms with all the amenities. Some larger rooms have a fully supplied kitchenette with fridge and stove. There is also a pool surrounded by a well-tended garden, private parking, laundry service, souvenir shop, travel agent and a babysitting service. Your breakfast and purified water is included in the price. The restaurant is open beam, with linen tablecloths, good service and home-made foods. This is a family-run establishment and their pride in excellence is obvious. The owners are friendly, helpful and knowledgeable about the area. They speak English and some German.

Miramar Paraiso Hotel, *Km 18 on the highway between San Blas and Puerto Vallarta,* ☎ *323-254-9030, www.sanblasyogaretreats.com, $$$*, is 20 minutes by bus from San Blas. This restored colonial mansion overlooks the ocean and has a path leading to the beach about 200 yards away. Two pools and palapa huts dots the lush grounds. There are six different styles of rooms, some with a balcony, some with extra-large windows and some that hold up to four people. All rooms have a private bathroom and shower. The Miramar is also a yoga retreat. Two yoga classes are offered daily: the morning

class is more strenu-
ous, while the evening
class focuses on medi-
tation and relaxation.
They also offer a jungle
survival course that
would be of interest to
anyone planning on
hiking in the tropics in
the future. Between
classes you can do
some exploring. The food is vegetarian and the lifestyle
conducive to losing weight. They encourage daily hiking,
Kombucha mushroom therapy and cleansing fasts. The
lady who does the mushroom therapy also teaches
dance, surfing and aerobics. Massage therapy is available. The owner does Huichol beadwork and will give lessons. Seven nights here, including meals and one
excursion per day (minimum of four people) is about
$1,200.

© San Blas Yoga Retreats

■ CAMPING

Los Cocos Trailer Park, *Batallon Rd, (1.5 km from
Zocalo),* ☎ *323-285-0055, $,* has 120 trailer pads with
hookups, plus an area designated for tenting, all tucked
into a coconut grove. There are hot showers and the popular Coco Loco Bar.

PLACES TO EAT

El Delfin, *at Hotel Garza Canela,* ☎ *323-285-0610, 1-9
pm,* is extremely clean and the water is safe to drink. The
cost for a dinner is about $10 per serving. This is a first-
class restaurant and should be tried at least once – for
that special night out. If you are tired of seafood, the
steak here is excellent.

La Familia, *Calle Batallon #18,* ☎ *323-285-0258,* is best
for dinner. Their seafood is famous – try their fried snap-
per. The décor is totally Mexican and the service is down-
home friendly.

South of Mazatlan

McDonald's, *Calle Juarez #35, 7 am-10 pm*, offers hamburgers that are nothing like the US chain version. These actually have tons of meat in them. Other meals are offered, too, but nothing that stands out. This is a popular place, which means the food is tasty and nobody gets sick from eating it.

Wala Wala, *Juarez #29, 8 am-10 pm daily except Sunday.* People come here for the fresh uncooked vegetables (they are safe to eat as they are washed in purified water). This, too, is a popular place, in part because of its simplicity and sparkling cleanliness. Meals cost under $10.

El Pescadito, *Calle Juarez and Canalizo,* is on the plaza. It comes highly recommended, although I didn't try it.

El Cocodrilario, *Calle Juarez and Canalizo, 8 am-10 pm.* The specialty here is spaghetti for $8 per serving. They have large servings and good service.

The Bakery, *Calle Cuauhtemoc,* around the corner from Posada del Rey, is the place to try great Mexican chocolate that has been baked into interesting cakes, cookies and tarts.

Appendix

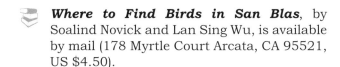

RECOMMENDED READING

■ NATURE

Where to Find Birds in San Blas, by Soalind Novick and Lan Sing Wu, is available by mail (178 Myrtle Court Arcata, CA 95521, US $4.50).

Where to Watch Birds in Mexico, Steve Howell, A&C Black Publishers, 1999. Covers 100 sites and about 1,000 species.

Guide to the Birds of Mexico and Northern Central America, Steve Howell, Oxford Press, 1995. Describes 1,070 species and covers Mexico and Central America down to northern Nicaragua. The guide features 71 color plates, plus maps.

Chasing Monarchs: Migrating with the Butterflies of Passage, Dr. Robert Michael Pyle, Houghton-Mifflin, 2001.

■ HISTORY

Heroic Defense of Mezcala Island, by Alberto Santoscoy is available as an e-book at www.epmassoc.com/catalog/175.php?sp=3. If this link is broken, type in the book title in your search engine to find another link. The book is an account of the fight between the people living on Mezcala Island and the Spanish.

GLOSSARY

THE CALENDAR

dia	day
semana	week
mes	month
año	year
domingo	Sunday
lunes	Monday
martes	Tuesday
miercoles	Wednesday
jueves	Thursday
viernes	Friday
sabado	Saturday
enero	January
febrero	February
marzo	March
abril	April
mayo	May
junio	June
julio	July
agosto	August
septiembre	September
octubre	October
noviembre	November
diciembre	December

NUMBERS

uno	one
dos	two
tres	three
cuatro	four
cinco	five
seis	six
siete	seven
ocho	eight
nueve	nine
diez	ten
once	eleven
doce	twelve
trece	thirteen
catorce	fourteen
quince	fifteen
dieciséis	sixteen

diecisiete . . . . seventeen
dieciocho . . . . eighteen
diecinueve . . . . nineteen
veinte . . . . twenty
veintiuno . . . . twenty-one
veintidós . . . . twenty-two
treinta . . . . thirty
cuarenta . . . . forty
cincuenta . . . . fifty
sesenta . . . . sixty
setenta . . . . seventy
ochenta . . . . eighty
noventa . . . . ninety
cien . . . . hundred
ciento uno . . . . one hundred one
doscientos . . . . two hundred
quinientos . . . . five hundred
mil . . . . one thousand
mil uno. . . . . one thousand one
dos mil . . . . two thousand
millón. . . . . one million
primero. . . . . first
segundo . . . . second
tercero. . . . . third
último . . . . last

■ CONVERSATION

¿Como esta? . . . . How are you?
¿Bien, gracias, y usted? . . . . Well, thanks, and you?
¿Que pasa?. . . . . What's happening?
Buenas dias. . . . . Good morning.
Buenas tardes. . . . . Good afternoon.
Buenas noches. . . . . Good evening/night.
Nos vemos. . . . . See you again.
¡Buena suerte!. . . . . Good luck!
Adios. . . . . Goodbye.
Que la vaya bien . . . . Goodbye (for someone special)
Mucho gusto. Glad to meet you.
Felicidades. . . . . Congratulations.
Feliz compleaños. . . . . Happy birthday.
Feliz Navidad. Merry Christmas.
Feliz Año Nuevo.. . . . . Happy New Year.
Gracias. . . . . Thank you.
Por favor. . . . . Please.
De nada/con mucho gusto. . . . . You're welcome.
Perdoneme. . . . . Pardon me (bumping into someone).

Permitame . . . . Pardon me (passing in front of someone).
Desculpe . . . . Excuse me (interrupting conversation).
¿Como se dice esto?. . . . . What do you call this?
Lo siento. . . . . I'm sorry.
Quiero... . . . . I want/I like...
Adelante. . . . . Come in.
Permitame presentarle... . . . . May I introduce...
¿Como se nombre?. . . . . What is your name?
Me nombre es... My name is...
No se. . . . . I don't know.
Tengo sed. . . . . I am thirsty.
Tengo hambre. . . . . I am hungry.
Soy gringa/gringo. . . . . I am an American (female/male).
¿Donde hay...?. . . . . Where is there/are there...?
Hay... . . . . There is/are
No hay. . . . . There is none
¿Que es esto? . . . . What is this?
¿Habla ingles? . . . . Do you speak English?
¿Hablan ingles? . . . . . . Is there anyone who speaks English?
Hablo/entiendo un poco . . . . I speak/understand a little
    Español . . . . Spanish.
Le entiendo. . . . . I understand you.
No entiendo. . . . . I don't understand.
Hable mas despacio por favor. . . . . Please speak more slowly.
Repita por favor. Please repeat.
¿Tiene...? . . . . Do you have...?
Tengo... . . . . I have...
Hecho... . . . . I make/made
¿Puedo?. . . . . Can I?
¿Permite me? . . . . May I?
La cuenta por favor. . . . . The bill, please.
bolsa . . . . bag
muchila . . . . backpack

TIME

¿Que hora es?. What time is it?
Son las... . . . . It is...
... cinco. . . . . five o'clock.
... ocho y diez. ten past eight.
... seis y cuarto. . . . . quarter past six.
... cinco y media. . . . . half past five.
... siete y menos cinco. . . . . five of seven.
antes de ayer. . . . . the day before yesterday.
anoche. . . . . yesterday evening.
esta mañana. . . . . this morning.
a mediodia. . . . . at noon.

en la noche. . . . . in the evening.
de noche. . . . . at night.
mañana en la mañana . . . . tomorrow morning.
mañana en la noche. . . . . tomorrow evening.

DIRECTIONS

Llevame alla ... por favor. . . . . Take me there please.
¿Cual es el mejor camino para...? . Which is the best road to...?
Derecha. . . . . Right.
Izquierda. . . . . Left.
Derecho/directo. Straight ahead.
¿A que distancia estamos de...? . . . . How far is it to...?
¿Es este el camino a...? . . . . Is this the road to...?
¿Es cerca? . . . . Is it near?
¿Es largo? . . . . Is it a long way?
¿Donde hay...? . . . . Where is... ?
... el telefono. . . . . the telephone.
... el baño. . . . . the bathroom.
... el correos. . . . . the post office.
... el banco. . . . . the bank.
...casa de cambio . . . . the money exchange office.
... estacion del policia. . . . . the police station.

ACCOMMODATIONS

¿Que quiere?. . . . . What do you want?
Quiero un hotel... . . . . I want a hotel that's...
... buena. . . . . good.
... barato. . . . . cheap.
... limpio. . . . . clean.
¿Dónde hay un hotel buena? . . . . Where is a good hotel?
¿Hay habitaciones libres? . . . . Do you have available rooms?
¿Dónde están los baños/servicios?. . Where are the bathrooms?
Quiero un habitacion . . . . I would like a room.
habitacion sencillo. single room.
habitacion con baño privado. . . . . . room with a private bath.
habitacion doble. double room.
baño comun . . . . . without a private bath/with a shared bath
ducha. . . . . shower
¿Esta incluido?. Is that included?
¿Puedo verlo? . . . . May I see it?
cama . . . . bed
cama matrimonial. double bed
¿Algo mas? . . . . Anything more?
¿Cuanto cuesta? . . . . How much?
¡Es muy caro! . . . . It's too expensive!

■ FOOD

```
comer . . . . . . . . . . . . . . . . . . . . . . . . . . . . . . . . . . . to eat
pan . . . . . . . . . . . . . . . . . . . . . . . . . . . . . . . . . . . . bread
carne . . . . . . . . . . . . . . . . . . . . . . . . . . . . . . . . . . . meat
papas . . . . . . . . . . . . . . . . . . . . . . . . . . . . . . . . . potatoes
leche . . . . . . . . . . . . . . . . . . . . . . . . . . . . . . . . . . . . milk
frutas . . . . . . . . . . . . . . . . . . . . . . . . . . . . . . . . . . . fruit
jugo . . . . . . . . . . . . . . . . . . . . . . . . . . . . . . . . . . . . juice
huevos . . . . . . . . . . . . . . . . . . . . . . . . . . . . . . . . . . eggs
mantequilla . . . . . . . . . . . . . . . . . . . . . . . . . . . . . . butter
queso . . . . . . . . . . . . . . . . . . . . . . . . . . . . . . . . . . cheese
agua mineral . . . . . . . . . . . . . . . . . . . . . . . . mineral water
cerveza . . . . . . . . . . . . . . . . . . . . . . . . . . . . . . . . . . beer
pescado . . . . . . . . . . . . . . . . . . . . . . . . . . . . . . . . . . fish
helado . . . . . . . . . . . . . . . . . . . . . . . . . . . . . . . ice cream
arroz . . . . . . . . . . . . . . . . . . . . . . . . . . . . . . . . . . . . rice
ensalada . . . . . . . . . . . . . . . . . . . . . . . . . . . . . . . . salad
jamon . . . . . . . . . . . . . . . . . . . . . . . . . . . . . . . . . . . ham
pollo . . . . . . . . . . . . . . . . . . . . . . . . . . . . . . . . . chicken
toronja . . . . . . . . . . . . . . . . . . . . . . . . . . . . . . grapefruit
naranja . . . . . . . . . . . . . . . . . . . . . . . . . orange (the fruit)
mariscos . . . . . . . . . . . . . . . . . . . . . . . . . . . . . . seafood
sopa . . . . . . . . . . . . . . . . . . . . . . . . . . . . . . . . . . . soup
vino tinto . . . . . . . . . . . . . . . . . . . . . . . . . . . . . red wine
vino blanco . . . . . . . . . . . . . . . . . . . . . . . . . . white wine
```

CONSULATES

■ AMERICAN

Acapulco, Hotel Continental Plaza, ☎ 744-484-0300 or 485-7207. Call only for specific emergencies.

Hermosillo, Edificio Sonora, Planta Baja, ☎ 662-217-2375, Monday to Friday, 9 am-5 pm.

Mazatlan, Playa Gaviotas #202, across from Hotel Playa Mazatlan, ☎ 669-916-5889, Monday to Friday, 8 am-4 pm.

Nogales, Calle Campillo, Edificio del Estado, 2nd Piso, ☎ 631-913-4820, Monday to Friday, 8 am-4:30 pm.

Puerto Vallarta, Zaragoza #160, Vallarta Plaza, ☎ 322-222-0069, Monday to Friday, 10 am-2 pm.

AUSTRIAN

Acapulco, Calle de Juan R. Escudero #1, 1st floor, ☎ 744-482-5551, Monday to Friday, 9 am-noon.

AUSTRALIAN

Mexico City, Ruben Dario #55, Col. Polanco, ☎ 555-101-2200, Monday-Thursday, 8:30 am to 5:15 pm; Friday, 8:30 am-2:15 pm.

BRITISH

Acapulco, Costera Miguel Aleman, ☎ 744-484-1735. This is an honorary consulate, so calling to make an appointment is necessary.
Mexico City, Lerma 71, Col. Cuauhtemoc, ☎ 555-242-8500, Monday-Thursday, 8 am-4 pm; Friday, 8 am-1:30 pm.

CANADIAN

Acapulco, Centro Comercial Marbella, ☎ 744-484-1306, Monday to Friday, 9 am-5 pm.

Mazatlan, Playa Gaviotas, # 202, ☎ 669-913-7320, Monday to Friday, 9 am-1 pm.

Puerto Vallarta, Zaragoza #160, Vallarta Plaza, ☎ 322-222-5398, Monday to Friday, 1-4 pm.

FINNISH

Mexico City, Monte Pelvoux 111, 4th floor, Lomas de Chapultepec, ☎ 555-540-6036. Call for hours of operation.

FRENCH

Mexico City, Lafontaine 32, Col. Polanco, ☎ 555-171-9840, Monday to Friday, 9 am-noon and 3:30-6:30 pm.

GERMAN

Mexico City, Lord Byron #737, Col. Polanco, ☎ 555-283-2200, Monday to Thursday, 7:30 am-3:30 pm; Friday, 7:30 am-3 pm.

ITALIAN

Acapulco, Gran Via Tropical #615-B, ☎ 744-481-2533. Call for hours.

Mexico City, Paseo de las Palmas, ☎ 555-596-3655. Call for hours.

JAPANESE

Mexico City, Paseo de la Reforma #295, 3rd floor, Col. Cuauhtemoc, ☎ 555-202-7900. Call for hours.

NEW ZEALAND

Mexico City, José Luis Lagrange #103, 10th floor, Col. Los Morales, ☎ 555-283-9460, Monday to Thursday, 8 am-4 pm; Friday, 8 am-1:30 pm.

SWISS

Mexico City, Torre Optima, Av. De las Palamas #405, Col. Lomas de Chapultepec, ☎ 555-853-5520, Monday to Friday, 9 am-noon.

Index

T

Tamazula, mission town, *153, 156*

Taxes and tipping, *72*

Teacapán, *174-176; accommodations, 175-176*

Tecuitata Waterfalls, *181-182*

Tennis: *Mazatlan, 122*

Tepic, *159-165; accommodations, 170-172; adventures, 165-170; city seal, 161; Environmental Education Ctr, 167; getting here, 159-160; history, 160-161; nightlife, 174-175; restaurants, 173-174; services, 162; sightseeing, 162-165*

Tequila, *26*

Tequila production, *131-132, 134*

Tipping, *72*

Toilets and toilet paper, *74*

Travel information, *47-88; communications, 69-71; consulates, 491-493; cultural*

tips, 72-73; documents, 50-53; facts, 47-48; gays and lesbians, 80; health, 56-63; money, 63-65; packing list, 53-56; pets, 53; police, 69; safety and security, 67-68; special needs, 72; toilets, 68; what to take, 50-56; when to go, 48-50

Tsunamis, *21-22*

Turtles, *35-37; San Blas, 183*

V

Value added tax, *72*

Volcán Ceboruco, *165*

W

Water, drinking, *62-63*

Whales, *42-43;*

Y

Yoga, *San Blas, 190-191*

Z

Zipolete, *80*